Shoot Like the Pros

The Road to a Successful Shooting Technique

Adam Filippi

TRIUMPH
BOOKS

Filippi, Adam.
  Shoot like the pros : the road to a successful shooting technique / by Adam Filippi.
     p. cm.
  ISBN 978-1-60078-546-7
  1. Basketball—Offense. 2. Basketball—Training. I. Title.
  GV889.F55 2011
  796.323'2—dc22

2010051134

This book is available in quantity at special discounts for your group or organization. For further information, contact:

Triumph Books
542 South Dearborn Street
Suite 750
Chicago, Illinois 60605
(312) 939-3330
Fax (312) 663-3557
www.triumphbooks.com

Printed in U.S.A.
ISBN: 978-1-60078-546-7
Design by Patricia Frey

Front cover photo by Christian Petersen/Getty Images. Back cover photo by AP Images.

Photos courtesy of Roberto Serra unless otherwise indicated. Models are German Scarone, Michael Fey, and Adam Filippi.

All diagrams courtesy of Fast Model Software, except diagrams on pages 115 and 116, which are courtesy of Daniele Zampogna.

To my beautiful daughters, Jade, Amber, and Ally…
my very own "triple threat"

Contents

Foreword

Over the years, I have watched thousands of basketball players of all ages. I've seen the game evolve and a few things have jumped out at me: tremendous ball-handling skills, more coaching at younger stages of players' careers, and the increased number of games played even before players reach high school. I marvel at the intensity and the work ethic of these young players, but I also see their frustration level when it comes to shooting. The single skill that is overlooked, and frankly not taught, is the art and technique of shooting.

In my youth, I didn't have any of the resources that young players have today to improve and to play against other gifted players. Having coaches and the opportunity to play in organized leagues gives them such an advantage to achieve early success. Unfortunately, many players overlook the most important skill and probably the one most difficult to master: shooting.

Striving for and mastering the ability to shoot on target consistently is almost impossible without the proper fundamentals. It takes a very dedicated athlete to comprehend the intricate yet simple art of shooting. I must caution everyone who reads this book that there might be more than one way to shoot the ball, but the fundamentals will always be similar.

Adam has done a great job of illustrating in his book how to grasp the fundamental skills and techniques necessary to make shots on a consistent basis; it is a book that warrants the attention of players and coaches at all levels.

I hope that you find this book as informative as I have: from the mechanics of shooting to the workout drills, everything about how to *Shoot Like the Pros* is addressed.

—**Jerry West**
Basketball Hall of Fame 1980 and 2010

Preface

I can remember sitting in the stands at NBA predraft camps watching most of the best college seniors go through spot-up shooting drills. And out of the 60 participating, I could never find more than a handful of players with good, consistent shooting techniques. As a basketball scout I became obsessed with analyzing players' shooting mechanics, noticing minor flaws that in many cases could be easily corrected with some simple adjustments. I began watching shooting videos, reading books on the skill, and exchanging ideas and concepts with various coaches around the world. In the meantime, I taught shooting at basketball camps and began working individually with players of all levels—from NBA to youth—who wanted to polish their techniques. I feel like I have studied and analyzed the art of shooting a basketball for the greater part of my life: first as a player, then as a professional scout, and now as a player development coach.

One day as I was preparing the content for an article on basketball fundamentals while waiting for my flight in a Paris airport, I realized that I could not stop writing about shooting. One thought led to another, one aspect had to be divided into several parts, and suddenly I had written a dozen pages and I still couldn't stop. There are just so many aspects to this fundamental skill. When I got home, I reviewed the many notes and concepts I had gathered through the years and kept on writing. So instead of the article, I decided to write a book dedicated exclusively to shooting. When I talk about shooting, I could address an almost infinite number of scenarios. In this book, however, we will try to cover most aspects, situations, variations, and more.

I've structured the book into seven chapters: Chapter 1 stresses the importance of shooting mechanics, i.e., analyzing all shot components and aspects with specific details, from basic stationary form shooting to jump shooting. Chapter 2 addresses the mental side of shooting. I've dedicated Chapter 3 entirely to foul shooting, because I consider the free throw the *mother* of all shots; both the "ultimate mechanical shot" and "ultimate mental shot." It is the best setting for analyzing mechanics and finding a consistent technique to build confidence. In Chapter 4, we'll take what we learned in the three previous chapters to the game setting. Chapter 5 focuses on how to improve a player's body—physical strength and conditioning specifically with respect to shooting. Chapters 6 and 7 are written with coaches in mind and include teaching methods, personalization, and workout drills for advanced levels.

I learn something new about the game of basketball every day, whether it's from a veteran coach, a young coach, a professional player, or a young kid just beginning to play the game. It is my hope that this book will be of assistance to players, coaches, and anyone who simply loves the game of basketball.

Enjoy the book and good luck!

Acknowledgments

My entire life has been all about basketball. Although my playing career never reached the levels that I had hoped for and despite several knee injuries, I was still able to play semiprofessionally. But the knowledge and experiences I gathered through the years made it possible for me to turn my life's passion into my profession. Basketball is a great sport because the more you put into it, the more you get out of it. The game has given me everything: taken me around the world, given me the opportunity to meet different people and learn new cultures and languages, enabled me to have contact with coaches and players I would never have thought possible, and allowed me to work for a world championship team. My bicultural basketball background and experiences have had a huge effect on my job and have driven me to write this book. I love this game and am so thankful for the opportunities it has provided.

I would like to thank the following great basketball minds for taking their time to read and evaluate my work and offer their testimonials. First of all, my heartfelt thanks to Jerry West, a Hall of Fame player who took the NBA to new levels in the 1960s and later set the standard for executives in the world of sports,

for having honored me by writing this book's foreword. I could talk basketball all day, every day with him. Also, thanks to Phil Jackson, the greatest coach of all time in any sport. And Bill Sharman, the NBA's first great shooter, a Hall of Famer both as a player and coach, and above all, the greatest gentleman I've ever met. Many thanks to Jim Boeheim, another Hall of Famer and legendary coach of Syracuse University, and Mike D'Antoni, whom I grew up watching play for Milan in the '80s, and who later established himself as one of the best offensive-minded coaches on both sides of the world. I can't leave out Bill Bertka, my mentor and colleague for 10 years, who is the greatest assistant coach and player development coach we might ever see.

I would also like to thank the great current and former NBA players who lent their expertise by contributing their shooting tips to the book: Vlade Divac, Rudy Fernandez, Danilo Gallinari, Chuck Person, Craig Hodges, Chauncey Billups, Derek Fisher, Glen Rice, Kiki Vandeweghe, Ray Allen, and again Jerry West and Bill Sharman.

In addition, I would like to acknowledge a close friend of mine, Coach Roberto Breveglieri, whom I consulted often throughout the project;

and my brother-in-law German Scarone, a fine professional basketball player and shooter, who posed as the model for the instructional pictures. I also want to mention my friends and fellow Lakers scouts Irving Thomas, Kevin Grevey, Gary Boyson, Ryan West, and Ronnie Lester for their support and encouragement.

Last but not least, I want to thank the many players I have had the pleasure of working with during the past few years, who in many ways have taught me so much and without whom I could never have written this book.

Key to Diagrams

(s) Shooter

(s) Shooter with Ball

(s) Shot

(1) First Shot

(2) Second Shot

(3) Third Shot

(c) Coach

(c) Coach with Ball

(p) Passer

x   Defender

R   Rebounder

‖   Hand Off

o o   Shooter's Feet

△   Cone

----▶   Pass

⊢   Screen

⟶▶   Movement/Cut

∿∿▶   Dribble

Introduction

Shooting is the most important fundamental skill in the sport of basketball. Coaches might stress other areas more, but the purpose of the game is and always will be to put the ball in the basket. You might be limited in some aspects of your game, but if you can make shots you have a good chance of finding a spot on any team.

Despite shooting being the skill that players are most willing to practice, shooting technique is perhaps the least-taught fundamental of the game. Shooting percentages across the board (two-pointers, three-pointers, and free throws) are dropping every year at all levels. Here are some possible reasons:

- More athletic and physical defenders in today's game
- Too much emphasis on playing five-on-five rather than working on fundamentals
- High school and college seasons are short. Most practice time is dedicated to team offense, team defense, and strategies for winning the next game. Not enough time is dedicated to perfecting individual skills.
- Very few players will acknowledge the fact that they may need to correct a mechanical flaw in their technique. They live comfortably in denial and are not open to *change*.
- Coaches and players are intimidated by the entire procedure of changing a player's shot. Correcting a player's shot and developing a new technique is a complex process that requires dedication, time, patience, and even time off from playing five-on-five.
- Players and/or coaches might not have a strategy or program for improvement.

> "Basketball is an overcoached and undertaught game."
>
> —Hall of Fame coach **Pete Newell**

When I speak at basketball camps or to young players I'm working with, I ask them what they think is the main reason for poor shooting percentages. The most common answers are "concentration," "confidence," and "they don't practice." Although these are all good reasons, the main reason for poor shooting is simply poor shooting form—from youth levels all the way to the pros.

People think basketball players don't practice their shooting. In most cases, this is not true. While many players might not work on improving every aspect of their overall game, of all of basketball's fundamentals, shooting is no doubt the skill practiced the most. The question is: do they know how to practice?

Players of all ages and levels have the misconception that if they go to the gym and get in as many shooting repetitions as possible, let's say in one hour, they are working on their shot. This is true only to a point. While this is a good start, players should have a practice plan that addresses all of the components of becoming a better shooter. Whether they need to make mechanical corrections in their form, want to quicken their release, or want to perfect shooting off the dribble, players should follow some kind of strategy and progression in order to reach the improvements they desire.

Despite being the skill the majority of players enjoy practicing the most, shooting is also the skill players are most sensitive to and resistant to adjusting, let alone changing. Many players with poor form do not address the fact that they may need to correct a major or minor

Shooting **TIP**

"Learn the proper fundamentals, and then the more you practice, the more you will improve and succeed."
—Hall of Fame player and coach **Bill Sharman**

mechanical flaw in their technique. Therefore, the player is practicing poor and/or incorrect form over and over through repetition. This way of training can become counterproductive, actually hurting one's jump shot by repeating a bad habit over and over. In some cases players, streak shooters in particular, might be able to improve their shooting percentages and be able to make shots anyway. But they will never be as good as they could have been had they made the proper adjustments.

Don't expect to see results overnight. Becoming a good shooter takes time, patience, organization, knowledge, and a lot of hard work!

Shooting Progression Training Model

Three Stages of Training

1. Mechanics Practice
Mastering proper technique and correcting any mechanical flaws

2. Repetition Practice
Repeating the correct movement enables muscle memory to become automatic

3. Competitive Practice
Re-creating gamelike pressure shooting drills and challenges

"Practice doesn't make perfect, perfect practice makes perfect."

The Shooting Progression Training Model is useful to players and coaches as a reminder that improvement happens over time and in a progressive manner. Many players think that just because they practice they will get better. That is a good start, but true only to an extent. There must be a practice plan and an understanding of how the player should progress step by step. Shooters who adopt this model will go through all three stages of practice and see measurable improvements through each. Very young (15 years old and under) players' training should only be through Stages 1 and 2, and as they develop physically, mentally, and emotionally, they will progress into Stage 3. An advanced player with correct mechanics may skip Stage 1 and focus on Stages 2 and 3, although I believe that reviewing basic shot mechanics with form shooting warm-ups is always a good everyday practice habit. This Progression Training Model is applicable to any basketball fundamental, not just shooting.

Stage 1—Mechanics Practice
In this stage you will focus on basic shooting mechanics: balance, hand placement, alignment, and follow-through. This phase is not based on high-intensity training from a physical standpoint, but you will need a high level of concentration and dedication. This is the time when coaches can stop, analyze, and correct most effectively, as you are working at a slower pace. You will "educate" yourself in this period, learning all aspects of proper technique and realizing why you miss shots. This part can be very frustrating because initially you may struggle with changing and correcting your old shooting form. Initially, you might even regress as a shooter. So you must persevere, have patience, and believe progress will come as you work harder each day. As improvements become noticeable, your confidence will also grow. Once you master correct and consistent

shooting mechanics, your goal will be to make your shot as automatic as possible through repetition.

Stage 2—Repetition Practice
You have learned proper shooting technique and you have corrected any mechanical flaws in your form. Now you will see how correct technique and repetition through (perfect) practice lead to muscle memory and automatic execution. Your confidence increases in this stage of training as you begin to make shots consistently. Players are inclined to dedicate the majority of their time to this stage, but if you have a poor technique you are actually hurting your shot—by practicing a fundamentally flawed shot motion, you are ingraining bad mechanics into your muscle memory and only making it harder to achieve proper shooting form. You must make the corrections in Stage 1 before advancing to this stage. At the same time, if you remain in the repetition training phase, skipping Stage 3, you will never challenge yourself to become a successful shot maker in real games.

Shooting TIP

"Developing muscle memory through repetition is of key importance."

—Ray Allen

Stage 3—Competitive Practice
Mastering flawless technique and practicing a good number of repetitions each day will surely lead a player to become a good shot maker. But is this good enough to make you a successful shooter in real games where you will only have one second over a defender, or

2' of space, or have the pressure of hitting the game-winning shot? No! To become a great game shooter you must practice in gamelike situations. Many good shooters "get their reps in" and can make some shots in games but never develop the "killer instinct" that separates the great from the rest. I have always loved the phrase, "game shots from game spots at game speed." This is what you want to replicate in this stage. Competitive training is technically, mentally, emotionally, and physically challenging. You need to practice at the same intensity—or higher—that you'll find in games if you want to take your entire game to the next level. The Stage 1 shooting drills require thinking about all components as you learned and corrected them; in Stage 3 your shot should be automatic and you should no longer think as you shoot. You should just focus on your target.

Chapter 1

Shooting Mechanics

BUILDING PROPER TECHNIQUE

Like most basketball fundamentals, shooting begins with the feet and ends with the hands. So I will begin talking about their roles and positioning first, then address correct alignment, follow-through, and how proper rhythm keeps it all together. During mechanics training your goal should be to eliminate any mechanical flaws and find consistency to develop an automatic shooting technique. You will focus mostly on form shooting, stand still shooting (set shooting), free throw shooting, and slowly progress into jump shooting.

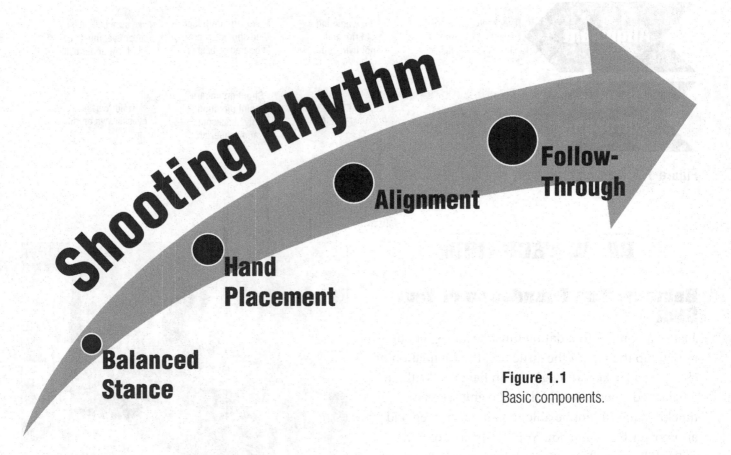

Shooting Rhythm

Balanced Stance

Hand Placement

Alignment

Follow-Through

Figure 1.1
Basic components.

Basic Shooting Mechanics Components	Two Basic Mechanical Parts
• Balance • Hands • Alignment • Follow-through	1. **Down**—Loading part: getting feet ready, flexing knees, cocking the ball, correct hand/arm positioning 2. **Up**—Pushing part: extension of all body parts—feet, legs, arms, upper body—in a coordinated sequence; wrist and finger flexion finishes the motion

Figure 1.2 Components and parts of basic shooting mechanics.

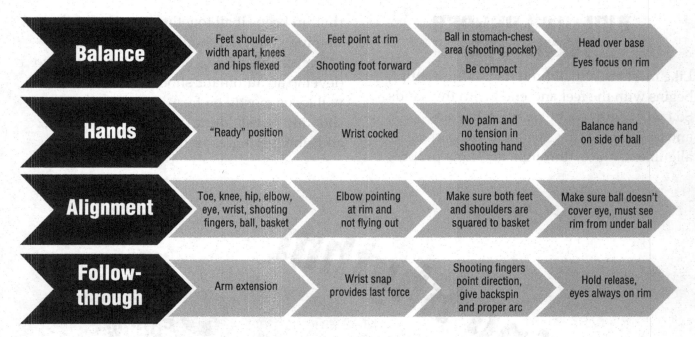

Balance	Feet shoulder-width apart, knees and hips flexed	Feet point at rim / Shooting foot forward	Ball in stomach-chest area (shooting pocket) / Be compact	Head over base / Eyes focus on rim
Hands	"Ready" position	Wrist cocked	No palm and no tension in shooting hand	Balance hand on side of ball
Alignment	Toe, knee, hip, elbow, eye, wrist, shooting fingers, ball, basket	Elbow pointing at rim and not flying out	Make sure both feet and shoulders are squared to basket	Make sure ball doesn't cover eye, must see rim from under ball
Follow-through	Arm extension	Wrist snap provides last force	Shooting fingers point direction, give backspin and proper arc	Hold release, eyes always on rim

Figure 1.3 Components of basic shooting mechanics.

BASIC TECHNIQUE

Balance: The Foundation of Your Shot

Just as a house's foundation must be strong enough to hold up the rest of the structure, the foundation of shooting a basketball begins with balance. Without a balanced stance, you will not be able to react quickly and will not be able to gain proper leg and arm power for your shot. You must stay compact with all body parts connected: legs, arms, shoulders, hands, head, and core.

Stance

Feet should be shoulder-width apart and pointing at the basket. If your feet are too close to each other, you will have no balance; if they are too wide, you won't be able to react. Weight should be equally distributed on both feet. Get your shooting toe (right or left, depending if you are right- or left-handed) aligned with the basket (see Figure 1.4). Some players tend to have their other foot pointed elsewhere. This causes hips to not be squared to the basket. You want both feet and 10

Figure 1.4. Stance.

Shooting **TIP**

"Foundation, form, and follow-through are the key components of a smooth shot."
—**Craig Hodges**

Craig Hodges' consistent form allowed him to win three consecutive NBA three-point contests from 1990 to 1992. (Photo by Andrew D. Bernstein/NBAE via Getty Images)

toes to the basket. Your legs must be flexed at the ankles and knees (don't overbend) because they provide the initial force in the shooting motion. Avoid keeping your weight on your heels. Keep your eyes on the rim.

Shooting Foot

Your shooting toe is aligned with the goal, pointing in the correct direction (shot line). You must compensate for the fact that you hold the ball on your strong side (right or left) as that shoulder will be slightly forward—although everyone says, "shoulders squared," that really isn't a natural position if you are holding the ball on one side. Therefore your lead foot should be slightly forward to balance your upper body. The back (nonshooting) foot's toe should be aligned with the instep of the shooting foot (see Figure 1.5). Don't let this slightly staggered foot stance twist your hips—they should still be as squared as possible to the rim.

Figure 1.5 Shooting foot.

Be Compact

You must eliminate any excess motion of arms, legs, and ball. You don't want to bend your legs too much or move the ball too much: unnecessary movement leads to increased chance for error. Hold the ball in your *shooting pocket*: the stomach-chest area closest to your center of gravity from where all movement begins, below shoulders, on your strong side (right or left). Keep elbows in—close to hips and shooting wrist already loaded (see Figure 1.6). You will find proper balance holding the ball in this region of the body, with your legs bent and ready to react. The combination of correct shooting pocket height (with wrist cocked) and proper use of legs provides the power to initiate the shooting motion. This concept is a very important aspect of your triple-threat stance.

Head and Shoulders

You must also be compact with your head. Leaning too far ahead, behind, or sideways—

Figure 1.6 Be compact.

Shooting **TIP**

"Your head position is key for your balance."

—**Jerry West**

out of your base of support—will cause you to lose balance. Feet and legs should provide a good base, with shoulders relaxed and not leaning back. Keep your head up with your eyes on the basket.

Hands: Correct Placement and Grip on the Ball

Hand placement is the most delicate part of your shooting form. Hand size and finger length affect your shot and positioning on the ball. We must address both shooting hand placement and balance hand placement. Find a comfortable grip on the ball: during the shot motion, your arms and hands should be in controlled tension—not too tight and not too soft.

Shooting Hand

The goal of the shooting hand is to make the ball go straight as you line up with the basket. You must develop correct, stable hand position to control the ball. You have to "feel" the ball: spread your fingers naturally and get a good grip. Don't try to palm the ball because this will cause too much tension—avoid too *wide* of a "V" between index and thumb. Don't keep your fingers too close because the ball will lay on your palm and you will have no control—avoid too *tight* of a "V" between index and thumb. You should be able to balance and control the ball with a good shooting hand grip, right above your shooting eye, approximately 90-degree angles at wrist and elbow (see Figure 1.7). Only your finger pads and thumb touch the ball. You

Figure 1.7 Shooting hand.

should be able to fit two fingers between the ball and palm to make sure there is no contact. When you snap your wrist to release the ball, don't close your hand because your rotation will be poor. Keep your fingers open—natural spread, no tension—with index and middle sending the ball in the correct direction.

Shooting **TIP**

"You cannot control the ball without a proper grip."

—**Derek Fisher**

> ### The Palm is Your Enemy!
>
> Remember you want *no palm* on the ball. Neither your shooting hand's nor your balance hand's palm should be in contact with the ball at any time. This rule not only applies to shooting, but also to dribbling and passing. This will allow you to control and feel the ball better, therefore making you a better ball handler and shooter.

Shooting Fingers: The "Shooting Fork"

The last fingers to touch the ball on its release determine the final force applied, direction, backspin, and "touch" on the shot. Not all players finish their shot the same way. Some may not even know which finger touches the ball last. Do you point at the basket with the index finger? Middle finger? Index and middle fingers? I insist that players release the ball off the two shooting fingers—index and middle, forming the "shooting fork"—especially since most people's middle fingers are significantly longer than their index fingers (see Figure 1.8). Position your two fingers in the middle of the ball forming a tight "V" (less than 1" between fingertips; the space in between should be the center of the ball. Practice using the ball's valve stem as point of reference—see Chapter 3: The Free Throw). The "two-shooting finger" technique provides the best control, backspin, and touch on the ball. However, this is very personal and there is no exact rule; you should choose for yourself depending on your feel on the ball. Whichever you choose, only three fingers (thumb, index, and middle) have a purpose in shooting the basketball. The two outside fingers (ring and pinky) are in contact with the ball only for stabilization and should not add any force to the shot.

Figure 1.8 "Shooting fork."

Wrist

Your shooting wrist should always be cocked back (almost a 90-degree angle with forearm; see a slight wrinkle in the skin), ready to shoot when you get in your "basketball stance." Even when you show your target for a pass, have your hands ready with wrist already cocked (see Figure 1.9). This might be difficult to do if a pass is poor and you have to reach for the ball, but get your hands in position immediately: wrist cocked, ready to shoot. Don't try to cock

Figure 1.9 Wrist.

the ball back as you raise it above your eye going up for your shot because this negative motion might cause the ball to slip backward out of your hands.

Balance Hand

You might hear the nonshooting hand referred to as the "help hand," "guide hand," or "off hand" (I do use this term). The best description, in my opinion is "balance hand," as its only purpose in shooting is to provide stability while raising the ball during the shot motion. The hand then must gently come off at your release point—the forehead area, above your right or left eye. This hand should not play any part in the release of the ball. It must give no force and no direction to the ball. Remember, you want a clean shot release. The balance hand should be on the *side* of the ball, not under and not in front (see Figure 1.10). Balance hand influence is probably the most common flaw in shooting mechanics; turning your thumb so that it pushes the ball and providing side spin, for example. It doesn't help the shot; it doesn't guide the ball anywhere. Don't let the balance hand put pressure on the ball and make sure it comes off as the shooting arm extends to thrust the ball. You can practice this motion, making the shooting hand and ball slide up and through the off hand without allowing any friction/dragging. Remember

Figure 1.10 Balance hand.

to end the shooting motion with the balance hand and fingers pointing up, opening the gate for the ball as the shooting arm extends. As with the shooting hand, the balance hand has no palm on the ball. Also, don't let the nonshooting arm and hand drop as your shooting arm extends because this movement will cause an imbalance/twist or jerk in your upper body, thus affecting the ball's direction.

Most Frequent Flaws Caused by the Balance Hand

- Balance hand turns and thumb (thumbing) pushes the ball, causing side spin.
- Balance hand is in front of the ball, not allowing a clean release. Open the gate! Finish with fingers up to the sky.
- Balance-hand fingers drag on the ball. You could be taking the hand off too late or it is

fall out of the alignment. This will result in a misdirected shot. Keep in mind that the absolutely perfect shot delivery is an ideal. There are some subtle variances among the great shooters, but the farther you stray from strict alignment principles, the less likely you are to become a consistently good shooter.

Shooting alignment components are the following body parts—right side if right-handed, left side if left-handed:

- Toe
- Knee
- Elbow
- Wrist
- Ball

Your *shot line* is determined by all of the above components being aligned in the same vertical plane with the strong side hip, eye, and the middle of the basket (see Figure 1.11).

Kobe Bryant shows a clean one-hand release with the balance-hand fingers pointing up to the sky. (Photo by Noah Graham/NBAE via Getty Images)

providing too much pressure on the side of the ball.
- Balance hand is under the ball, almost touching the shooting hand and exerting unwanted force on the ball.
- Balance-hand palm is in contact with the ball.

Alignment

The alignment principle is easy to understand and hard to disagree with. Still, many players let one component fall out of line, which consequently affects the other alignment parts. This results in what I refer to as a *broken alignment*. Very common example: if your shooting elbow is out of line (a flying elbow) this will change your hand position on the ball, and your wrist and shooting fingers will

Figure 1.11 Alignment.

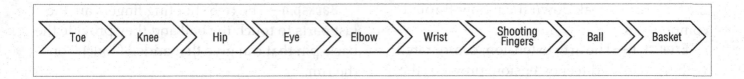

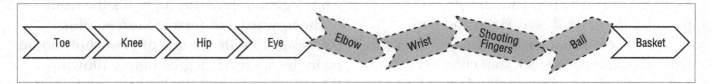

Figure 1.12 Proper alignment.

Alignment Points

- Proper alignment determines your shot line to the middle of the basket.
- Your shooting toe must point to the rim.
- Your shoulders should be perpendicular to your shot line.
- Your shooting hand must be positioned correctly, with your "shooting fork" in the middle of the ball and already pointing in the direction of the rim.
- Elbow in—your elbow should be under the ball as much as possible. You must be comfortable, so if it is slightly out of line, that's okay, as long as it extends within the alignment as you release the ball.
- Ninety-degree angles—body and arm, forearm and upper arm, wrist and forearm all must be at approximately 90-degree angles. (You are not a robot and need to feel comfortable.)
- Your hips should be squared to the basket. If they turn and your shoulders remain squared, your elbow might not be able to get through due to friction with your side and might be forced to "fly out."
- At your release point, your shooting hand should be under the ball, not behind the ball.

- Don't raise the ball behind your head—your shot will be either too flat or too high.
- When in your basic basketball stance (triple threat), keep elbows in near your sides. Be compact.

Follow-Through: Finishing the Shot

To finish your shooting motion successfully, you must have proper follow-through. This final part of the shot begins as you have brought the ball up to your release point, above the eye as your legs straighten. Now you must smoothly extend your arm and snap your wrist (see Figure 1.13). These final two motions of your shot will give the last force (both upward and forward), direction, backspin, and arc to

Shooting **TIP**

"*The quality of my follow-through tells me if the shot is going in before it actually does.*"

—Derek Fisher

the ball. Let's break down the follow-through components:

Extension—The arm extension, coordinated with the legs and feet extension, provides the *upward force*.

Wrist Snap—The hand and finger flexion provides the *forward force*. Hand and wrist should be somewhat relaxed. You don't want a tense shot, but not a weak shot either. The snap can't be too sharp, because should you hit the front rim, it will probably bounce off instead of rolling in softly.

Direction—The two shooting fingers, index and middle, will give the ball the correct direction as the wrist snaps. Fingers must point down at the end of the snap. I like to say, "put the two shooting fingers into the rim."

Figure 1.13 Follow-through.

Backspin—The two shooting fingers are the last parts to touch the ball and they provide the backspin that can give that added "touch" on the rim.

Arc—A good and high shooting arc comes from a good follow-through. It's the result of the upward and forward forces, plus backspin. The ideal angle of your shot should be in the 50- to 55-degree range, allowing the ball to drop into the basket from the sky down. Avoid pushing the ball: make sure you are within your shooting range and have correct shooting pocket and release point positions. *Make sure your shooting elbow extends at eye level.*

Eyes—Always focus on the rim as you follow through. Don't follow the ball's trajectory as you might move your head; any kind of head jerking (whether forward, back, or side) will affect your follow-through negatively. The only time you will be following the ball's rotation is when you are learning and analyzing shot mechanics.

Body Balance—Neither retract nor fall forward with your head and shoulders during the follow-through. End up in balance on your toes in stationary shooting and free throws (not in jump shooting) with your body just slightly forward as you finish your shot.

Confident shooters hold their follow-through (see Figure 1.14). They are so

Shooting **TIP**

"When I shoot, I never follow the flight of the ball in the air. I always keep my eyes focused on the rim."
—Danilo Gallinari

Figure 1.14 Hold your follow-through.

focused on the act of shooting and the rim that they might keep their hands up all the way back on defense. Holding your follow-through is a good habit not only for making shots, but also because it leaves *evidence* in your form. If you miss, you can look at your fingers and see that maybe the ball was released off the "ring and pinky" fingers, or you gave a right/left direction and not straight at the rim, or you didn't snap your wrist all the way down.

Also, a good follow-through can often *fix* mechanical errors in your shooting form.

> Picture Michael Jordan making the Bulls' 1998 Championship game-winning shot. How did he finish his shot? Holding his follow-through an extra two seconds after the ball had already gone in.

SHOOTING RHYTHM

Shooting Rhythm		
Leg Motion		**Arm Motion**
— *Balanced Stance*	*Coordination*	— *Shooting Pocket*
— *Knee Bend*		— *Release Point*
		— *Follow-Through*

Shooting **TIP**

"Rhythm is the most important thing for me. The better rhythm my body produces, the more I know my shot will go in."

—Danilo Gallinari

Danilo Gallinari is becoming one of the NBA's top long-range shooters. At 6'10" and with a quick release, he's almost impossible to block. (Photo by Gary Dineen/NBAE via Getty Images)

We've discussed and analyzed each segment of the shooting motion: feet, knees, elbow, arm, hand, and fingers. The binding force that keeps all the elements together in a fluid motion is *rhythm*. Legs, arms, shoulders, hands, head, and core must be connected in order to produce smooth mechanics. Rhythm is created through the coordination between your leg motion and your arm motion, allowing a fluid and comfortable shooting technique. Efficient leg and arm motions generate the needed power for your shot, so you don't have to search for additional strength with compensations (in Chapter 5 you will see how the core stabilizes the two motions). Your movements should be power-producing and excess-motion-saving.

Your legs begin the shot motion, providing the initial push. You must not raise the ball as you flex your knees, but keep it in your shooting pocket. When players raise the ball as they flex their knees, this can chop rhythm and momentum and slow down the motion. Remember that the coordination between your legs and arms is the key to a smooth motion. You want to be ready, in your basketball stance, with legs loaded, and have every element go up together. All angles open up in a fluid sequence. Shooting wrist and finger flexion (follow-through) ends the rhythmic motion. Head and shoulders must be relaxed. At the end of the shot, your body should be inclined very slightly forward, never falling back (negative motion).

Leg Motion

Good leg motion is determined by a solid balanced basketball stance and the proper use of your legs. Most adult players should have enough upper-body strength to shoot the basketball without the use of their legs. But without that initial knee flexion and leg push, you would not be able to create a fluid rhythm and would remain too stiff. This often happens with very tall players who might not necessarily need the power from their legs to reach the goal and want to eliminate excess motion. The results

Shooting TIP

"My main checkpoint is my legs. If I get my legs under me I know everything else will fall into place for making the shot."
—Glen Rice

are a choppy rhythm, stiff and robotic form, and poor shooting percentage. This is one of the reasons bigger players don't develop rhythm as easily as smaller ones and sometimes struggle at the free throw line. Players might use or need different levels of leg power, but even the tall or strong ones need a little knee flexion to produce a smooth shot. You should not *over*bend your knees because you don't want too much excess movement—be compact—that could lead to a mistake somewhere along the line. The longer the range of your shot, the more leg bend is necessary, but never more than a 45-degree angle maximum on any shot, as it will also slow it down.

As we talk about jump shooting and long-range shooting we'll see how more leg power and a stronger swinging motion of your arms will generate more momentum and elevation off the ground. Remember that the ball should leave your hand on your way *up*, not at the top of your jump.

Rhythm

In my experience, rhythm is the most difficult part of shooting to teach players. The reason is that a coach or teacher cannot feel what another person is feeling. Since personal coordination has a big role in the shooting motion, rhythm is a very subjective matter and it should develop within each individual player. You cannot expect each player to adapt to the same method of teaching.

Arm Motion

The arm motion complements the leg push to create more force and rhythm during the shot. From your balanced stance, you'll begin your leg push, transferring the ball from the *shooting pocket* to the *release point* (the two key ball positions), and then finish the shot with a good follow-through.

The Two Key Ball Positions

1. Shooting Pocket—The shooting pocket is the stomach-chest area, below your shoulders, on your strong side (right or left). Exact position might change depending on size, strength, and age, but the lower the pocket, the more power is achieved. Never dip the ball before you

Figure 1.15 Shooting pocket.

raise it to shoot. This is where your shot starts and where you hold the ball in your typical offensive basketball stance (triple threat), with your legs flexed. Be compact; keep the ball near your body (see Figure 1.15). You don't want to move the ball too much, exposing it to the defense and/or losing balance. In addition, holding the ball too far out in front of you will make you raise the ball with a backward force (negative motion) instead of an upward force. From this key position, you are *ball quick*: able to efficiently put the ball on the floor (straight or ripping it low to the other side), pass, fake a shot, or go straight into your shot. Don't hold the ball between your legs, and don't hold the ball high or behind your head; you are *not* a shooting threat in these positions. Proper shooting pocket combined with proper use of legs provides the power to initiate your shooting motion.

    2. Release Point—The other key ball position is the release point. This position is not where the ball is released from the fingers, but the area to where you raise the ball from your shooting pocket, just before the full extension of the shooting arm. The ideal release point is right above your eye/forehead on your shooting side, which allows you to see the basket properly from underneath the ball (see Figure 1.16). An incorrect release point can affect your rhythm, momentum, view, and shot quality. Since everyone has different physical tools (height, size, length of limbs, hands, age, etc.) players must make natural adaptations in their technique. Tall players with long arms tend to raise the ball higher or sometimes, even worse, way behind their heads—which can lead to either a very flat shot or an exaggerated arc. Weak, often younger, players usually have a lower point of release or just push directly from their shooting pocket in a single motion. They see the basket from above the ball and might have good form, but the shot might be

Figure 1.16 Release point.

easy to block at higher levels. As these players develop they will need to make adjustments. In any case, make sure you can see the basket properly with both eyes to avoid tilting or jerking your head during your follow-through.

Note: *Your shooting hand, wrist, and arm should never change position, remaining at approximate 90-degree angles as you raise the ball from the shooting pocket position up to your release point position.*

If we break shooting mechanics down, there are two synchronizations that occur. In between them there is a very brief pause (see Figure 1.17):

1. **Legs** (knees) extend as arms raise the ball from shot pocket to release point (ball in forehead area, above right eye if you are right-handed).

2. **Pause** (extremely brief— no hitch!): In set shooting and free throw shooting your motion should be so smooth and continuous that the pause barely occurs. The briefer the pause, the smoother the rhythm and the quicker the release.

3. **Ankles** extend (feet push off the ground giving force) as shooting arm extends and hand flexes, thrusting the ball.

Figure 1.17 Two synchronizations with a brief pause in between.

VISION AND AIM

See the Floor: Keep Your Head Up!

Coaches always stress the importance of players seeing the basket or keeping their eyes on the rim. I have never understood this concept. The basket doesn't move, but the other nine players on the floor do! A good player can continue seeing the basket with peripheral vision without focusing on it.

Perhaps the best jump shooter in the game today, Ray Allen has mastered all aspects of shooting fundamentals, from basic technique to moving without the ball, from shooting off the dribble to long-range shots. (Photo by Kent Smith/NBAE via Getty Images)

Shooting TIP

"Sometimes in games the defender may not allow me to see the rim properly, but I've practiced that shot over and over with the same intensity so the chances of that shot falling increase every time."

—Ray Allen

In any live basketball situation, whether you are dribbling, passing, shooting, or moving without the ball—on offense or defense— you must be able to see the floor. The ball moves quickly, and your teammates and your opponents are in constant motion. The object is to keep your head up and be alert, so as not to miss a scoring opportunity for your team. I want players to "see" the basket, but I really want them to see what's happening on the floor (teammates' positions, cuts, spacing, defensive adjustments, etc.).

It's true that "eyes on the rim" makes your defender think you are going to shoot and it might open up your drive. But simply squaring up to the basket within your shooting range should make you an immediate threat without having to look at the basket. Many times, focusing on the rim too long (staring at it) can cause you to overthink, hurting the automatism of your shot form.

The only time players need to keep their eyes focused on the rim is when they are actually performing the shot. As soon as they begin their shooting motion, their eyes should focus exclusively on the target.

See the Rim With Both Eyes When Shooting

Correct shooting mechanics should allow you to see the basket properly. After you raise the ball to your release point above your shooting eye, you should be able to comfortably see the goal underneath the ball, between your arms, with both eyes (see Figure 1.18).

Don't allow the ball, your hand, or arm to cover your view of the rim during your shot motion. Not seeing the basket properly will force you to either tilt your head or move your shooting hand to one side in order to see the goal, and this will negatively affect your shot. If you can't see the rim with both eyes, review your mechanics and check if you are aligned correctly.

Figure 1.18 See the rim with both eyes.

What Part of the Basket Should You Focus On?

The rim is your target from whatever angle you are shooting. You want to put the ball into the basket. What part of the rim should you aim at? Some coaches tell you to focus on the front of the rim, some on the back, some on the net's loops, some on the middle of the basket. I always found this to be a bit confusing, especially as a player. I have another concept: focus on the rim, but not on a particular part. Try to simply *visualize* a clear image of the ball right above the rim, dropping straight down through it: the mental picture of a perfect shot just before the ball goes through the net (see Figure 1.19). Every time you look at the rim you should automatically have this positive image, as it will also enhance your confidence (see Chapter 2, "The Mental Side"). Remember, however, that this is very subjective and the bottom line is this: focus where you feel the most comfortable and on whatever works for you.

Figure 1.19 Focus on the rim and mentally picture a perfect shot.

Bank Shots

Banking a shot off the glass is a different situation. Although your shooting form should not change when you are shooting a bank shot, your target is no longer the rim. Now you should aim for the upper corner of the white square on the glass. Most players tend to change their arc a bit while shooting off the glass, thus flattening it; this will cause a harder shot that has to be perfectly on target in order to go in. So try to keep proper arc and rotation in order to maintain a soft touch.

The change of your target from the middle of the rim to the upper corner of the box can cause some indecision right before your release, which is the last thing you want to occur. Therefore, I recommend using the help of the backboard only in certain situations, unless it involves a simple layup or shot around the hoop. Otherwise, limit its use to midrange shots from 12' to 15' and from a 45-degree angle. If you feel comfortable and are proficient using this shot in games, I advise you to include it in your daily repetitions.

PROGRESSING INTO THE JUMP SHOT

While the basic "stand-still" set shot technique is fundamentally the most correct shooting method, it also becomes more limited as you advance through each level of basketball, from the youth leagues to the pros.

The game has become so quick, athletic, and physical that the higher level you play, the fewer chances you will have to shoot a comfortable set shot. In order to advance as a player and thrive in real games, you must develop a jump shot.

One of the purest jump shooters in NBA history, Peja Stojakovic, shows his form. (Photo by Nathaniel S. Butler/ NBAE via Getty Images)

Young Players

You should progress into jump shooting only after you have already mastered a correct set shooting technique and have the necessary physical capabilities.

A lack of strength will cause you to shoot a jump shot with an incorrect form, which will eventually jeopardize your development as a shooter and overall player.

Your jump shot should have the same basic mechanics as your set shot and your free throw shot. The difference is the increase of power you provide to the motion and to the elevation with which you execute it. A stronger swinging motion of your arms, combined with more leg power, generates more momentum and elevation off the ground. Your feet are also of crucial importance because they should forcefully extend as your body uncoils. The ball should leave your hand right before the top of your jump. Avoid too long of a "hang time," any hesitation or stop at the peak of your jump will result in a "hitch" that will break your shooting rhythm and momentum. In addition, you will have a slower release and a more limited shooting range.

Repetitive jump shooting requires more energy than set shooting and will cause you to tire more quickly. That's why you must also prepare your body appropriately if you want to improve your jump shooting skills.

How Much Are You Supposed to "Jump" for a Good Jump Shot?

In some ways the answer to this question depends on what your physical and athletic abilities allow you to do. But in truth, you don't need to jump much or try to outjump the defender.

The farther the distance of the shot, the less you need to jump. Most players use more leg power combined with a lower shot pocket, but you do not need much lift off the ground because from long range you usually have more time to get your shot off.

The closer you get to the basket, the more you might need to jump and you might have to raise the ball slightly higher because you will be tightly guarded or in the heart of the defense.

Do You Shoot a Jump Shot or an "Elevation Shot"?

"Elevation shot" is a typical European basketball term to describe a shot many players use, perhaps without even realizing it. In my opinion, the best way to describe this shooting method is as a cross between a "set shot" and a "jump shot." You don't actually shoot during your "airtime," but instead shoot as you extend your body and release with your feet barely leaving the ground. You don't gain maximum height, but it is a pretty quick method that provides a smoother rhythm and might give you more range.

Landing—Land in balance. Don't fade sideways or backward. Don't try to imitate the All-Stars! While the idea is to land in the same spot you elevated from, it is okay that your body's natural momentum takes you slightly forward.

PLAYERS WITH LIMITED STRENGTH

Unfortunately, many young players with limited strength try to shoot from a high release point like they see the professionals do. This causes a number of strength compensations that can lead to several mechanical errors—broken alignment, balance-hand turn, choppy rhythm, etc. Any one of these flaws will lead to an incorrect technique and poor results, so it is better to make some simple mechanical adaptations until players have grown into their bodies or developed more strength.

Don't be afraid to lower your shooting pocket and point of release positions. This is the best method for overcoming a lack of upper-body strength because it allows you to develop a correct technique that will not require many adjustments as you grow bigger and stronger. On the contrary, poor methods like shooting with two hands or trying to shoot from above your head or from outside your shoulder might allow you to reach the goal better, but will not help your accuracy and you will develop a bad habit. In addition, this will complicate your entire shooting evolution even more as you grow older and gain strength, forcing you then to rebuild a completely new technique. It is much easier to adjust a lower shot technique to a higher one, than it is to entirely change a shot as a body matures.

Step-In Method

To gain more lower-body power you can add a *step-in* to your shooting motion. This is a two-count motion, as you first catch the ball with one foot back and then you step in, providing more leg force. Stay low with legs loaded and don't raise your hips as you step forward into the shot. Combining the step-in with a lower shooting pocket, you will gain more power and momentum for your shot while maintaining a

correct shot line (see Figure 1.20). This is a very efficient method for players of any age and level on long-range shots where there might be more time to prepare the shot. (See "Increasing Shooting Range" in Chapter 4.)

Figure 1.20 Step-in method.

Note: *For young kids, eight to 12 years old, I recommend shooting with a youth-size basketball and at an 8' or 9' basket. This will allow them to build a correct and comfortable shooting technique at a young age.*

Common Qualities in Good Shooters

1. **Balance**—Shoulders squared, knees flexed, weight distributed on both feet, head above base, "compact" with the ball. Good consistent footwork.
2. **Fluid one-hand technique**—No mechanical flaw in shooting arm/hand.
3. **Balance hand on side of the ball**—No pushing/dragging/turning by balance hand. Fingers straight and pointing up as hand comes off.
4. **Follow-through**—Finish shot motion with full extension and wrist snap and hold an extra couple of seconds.
5. **No left or right misses**—Only miss long or short. This means there is good alignment.
6. **Court sense**—Feel for the court, spots, angles, spacing, and timing, and ability to move without the ball.
7. **Good shot selection**—Know when and where there is a good shot. Know if there is a teammate in better position to shoot.
8. **Concentration**—While you begin the shot motion, remain focused on your target and don't allow outside distractions. Mechanics should be automatic; don't think about them too much.
9. **Confidence**—Think positively, remain sure of capabilities, visualize every shot going in.

Misses

A good shooter knows the reason for every miss. "I felt the ball go off my outside fingers not my two shooting fingers," "My elbow was out," "I didn't get enough push from my legs," etc. Then a shooter immediately erases the mistake, readjusts, and corrects form for the next shot.

Common Flaws in Technique — Reasons for Misses

- Balance-hand interference
- Poor direction from shooting fingers
- Flying elbow (broken alignment)
- Palm on ball (shooting hand or balance hand)
- Poor balance
- Fading left or right
- Lack of power
- Choppy rhythm
- Poor arc
- Release point too high or behind the head
- Poor follow-through
- Negative motion

Causes for Negative Motion (Backward Force)

- Leaning back
- Retracting shoulders (too stiff)
- Jerking your head back
- Hopping back, or fading, trying to imitate the NBA stars
- Raising the ball too far behind your head
- Cocking your wrist as you raise the ball instead of having it already in a "loaded" position as you catch it
- Holding the ball too far out in front of your body, instead of close in your shooting pocket, will make you raise the ball with a backward force instead of an upward and forward force.

Main Reasons for Missed Shots and Corrections

Left or Right Missed Shots	Short or Long Missed Shots

A good shooter tries to eliminate right/left misses.

Shooting hand is misplaced on the side of the ball and your release causes sidespin. Make sure that you hold the ball with the two shooting fingers in the middle of the ball and that when you reach your release point your hand is under the ball.

Shooting fingers flex right or left instead of straight toward the middle of the rim. As you snap your wrist, make sure the ball comes off your index and middle fingers and point in the correct direction.

Outside fingers (ring and pinky) were the last to touch the ball. Control the ball so that it lies mainly on thumb, index, and middle fingers, with these last two in the middle of the ball, releasing the ball toward the basket.

Flying elbow: Your elbow is not aligned with the toe, knee, wrist, and ball and not pointing at the rim. You must keep your elbow in at the side of your hip, and as you raise the ball it should be aligned underneath it.

Balance hand is the main cause for right/left misses. You might have misplaced it either in front of the ball so that it didn't allow a clean release; or you twisted your balance hand so that the thumb ended up pushing the ball so that it won't go straight. You must keep the nonshooting hand on the side with no tension and end with the hand and fingers pointing up and "opening the gate."

Poor balance: Maybe your legs are too close or too wide or your head is not above your base. Stay low; ankles, knees, and hips flexed; feet shoulder-width apart; weight equally distributed on both feet in a compact stance with the ball near your body.

Poor square up: Either spotting up or on the move, you don't get your body squared to the rim. This causes broken alignment. You must either pivot or hop into a balanced stance, shoulders and hips squared with 10 toes pointing at rim. Squaring up, you are automatically a threat!

Fading left or right: This happens especially on the move, when players are often out of control and can't regain balance, or they try to square up in the air. You must stay low as you receive the pass or pick up the ball from your dribble, gather yourself with proper footwork (inside pivot usually) that allows you to get shoulders and feet squared to the basket and go up for the shot.

Short and long misses are caused by a power problem.

Legs didn't provide enough force. Your lower body must initiate your shot motion. You must flex your ankles, knees, and hips to get proper power. Do not overbend your legs, though.

Shooting pocket is too high. You are not getting enough force from your arms. The lower your pocket, the more power you will achieve.

Broken rhythm: Your body extends in a choppy manner—a dip, a hitch, poor coordination between legs and arms—causing decreased power and fluidity. Begin with your legs flexed and extend them as you raise the ball in a smooth motion.

Poor extension: You might get proper force from your legs and possibly even your wrist snap, but you don't extend your shooting arm completely. You must extend it up so that your elbow ends above your eyes.

Poor arc: Either too low (flat) or too high. Make sure your palm isn't on the ball and that you follow through, giving an up-and-forward force. Don't bring the ball behind your head at release point. Your elbow should end above eye level.

Late release: Don't shoot at the peak of your jump; don't hang in the air too long and shoot on your way down; don't keep too high of a release point. Shoot on your way up as your body extends in a rhythmic motion.

Poor follow-through: You don't finish your shot, so you don't give that last amount of force and backspin/touch. Extend your arm and snap your wrist, releasing the ball off of the shooting fingers. Hold your arm up until the ball reaches the goal. At the free throw line you should end up on your toes, in balance.

Negative motion: You might retract your shoulders, fade backward, or raise the ball behind your head. These motions will cause your body to move in one direction while the ball is being pushed in the opposite direction (force struggle). You must keep your shoulders relaxed, release the ball above your shooting eye, and jump up and slightly forward. It's better to land one foot forward rather than backward. At the free throw line, your head, chest, and shoulders should end slightly forward while you balance yourself on your toes without stepping over the line.

Note: One or more of these mistakes can occur when shooting on the move and off the dribble, usually with close defensive pressure because you might be forced to accelerate your shot or shoot off balance. Often this happens when squaring up in the air and you end up fading sideways. You could end up holding the ball incorrectly and you may put too much tension or pressure on it during your release. This should never occur at the free throw line because you have plenty of time and no defense.

SHOOTING MECHANICS DRILLS

Perform drills starting close to the basket and move out progressively. If you are a beginner or are working to make adjustments to your shooting technique, you might need to begin "away from the basket," shooting the ball straight up in the air to yourself (see Figure 1.21). As you feel more comfortable and confident in your new mechanics, perform using the basket.

Form Shooting Drills

One-Hand Form Shooting Drill

This drill improves your ability to control the ball, your feel for it, and proper one-hand release. Practice this in your basic basketball stance, in balance, with legs and hips flexed and the ball in your shooting pocket area. There are two versions:

1. Feel the ball as it lays in your shooting hand and find a good grip. Then raise the ball up to your release point, rotating your hand and forearm to the correctly aligned shooting position (See Figure 1.22). Keep your shoulders squared and shoot the ball. Hold your follow-through.
2. Use your balance hand to help prepare the shot while holding the ball in your shot pocket. Find the proper grip, and with your shooting hand only, raise the ball up to your release point. Keep your shoulders squared and shoot the ball. Hold your follow-through.

Shooting to Yourself Away from the Basket

Shooting the ball to yourself away from the basket allows you to focus exclusively on the correct mechanics without the pressure of converting the shot. This way, you avoid feeling discouraged and doubtful of your new shooting technique until you have mastered it and it becomes automatic.

Although there is not a rim involved, you should always use your imagination to visualize a perfect shot with the ball swishing through the net.

Figure 1.21 Shooting to yourself.

Figure 1.22. One-hand form shooting drill.

Your goal in both versions of this drill is to make the ball go straight to the basket as you have no balance-hand interference. Knowing that you have eliminated right and left misses will boost your confidence in your shooting technique.

Progression: Shoot to yourself, away from the basket, and then shoot at the basket. Begin at close range and then move back.

One-Hand Form Shooting with Balance Hand Drill

Use your balance hand to prepare the shot and raise the ball up to your release point. Take the nonshooting hand off of the side of the ball, keeping that arm up, and release the ball one-handed with a good follow-through (see Figure 1.23).

Progression: Shoot to yourself, away from the basket, and then shoot at the basket. Begin at close range and then move back.

Figure 1.23 One-hand form shooting with balance hand drill.

Two-Hand Form Shooting Drill

Same as the previous drill, but now with your regular shooting form, using both hands. Release the ball, making sure that you use a clean one-hand release, avoiding any balance-hand interference (see Figure 1.24).

Progression: Shoot to yourself, away from the basket, and then shoot at the basket. Begin at close range and then move back.

Figure 1.24 Two-hand form shooting drill.

On Your Back Shooting Drill

Lie on your back with the ball positioned right above your strong-side armpit, your shooting elbow on your side (it's okay if it touches the floor), and your hands/fingers in correct position with shooting wrist already cocked. Release the ball vertically up in the air, letting it fall straight back into your hands in their original position (see Figure 1.25). Focus on extending your shooting arm straight up with good follow-through, wrist snap, and backspin. Almost every aspiring player has tried this while lying in bed fantasizing about making a big shot!

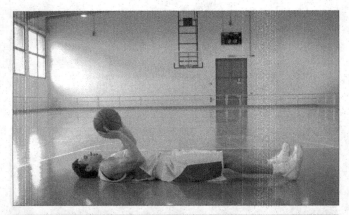

Figure 1.25 On your back shooting drill.

Chair Shooting Drill

Sit in a chair with your back straight. Begin close to the basket (5' range) and move back progressively. Prepare your shot with correct hand placement and proper alignment in your shooting pocket, then shoot the ball—extending your arm with a good follow-through (see Figure 1.26). This drill will make you rely on the strength of your back, shoulders, shooting arm, and wrist, so you will exaggerate your follow-through. As a result, you will also improve your shooting range.

Progression: Shoot to yourself, away from the basket, and then shoot at the basket. Begin at close range and then move back—never to a distance so far that you must alter your technique by straining yourself or throwing the ball, compromising your shot line.

Figure 1.26 Chair shooting drill.

Floor Shooting Drill

This drill is a progression from the chair shooting drill as now you are further challenged by sitting on the floor with your legs either crossed or open (see Figure 1.27). Only players with the appropriate upper-body strength should utilize this drill. Perform following the same guidelines as in the chair shooting drill.

Progression: Shoot to yourself, away from the basket, and then shoot at the basket. Begin at close range and then move back— never to a distance so far that you must alter your technique by straining yourself or throwing the ball, compromising your shot line.

Figure 1.27 Floor shooting drill.

Shooting Balance Drills

These "hop drills" are designed to develop proper body balance and control while shooting the ball. In addition, they improve overall body coordination and shooting rhythm to build a fluid shot motion. Perform these drills from midrange, using a two-foot hop in the following patterns and combine with the ball positions described below:

- **Stationary hops**—Three hops in the same spot, shooting on the last one
- **Forward hops**—Three forward hops, shooting on the last one
- **Side hops**—Three hops to one side, shooting on the last one
- **Forward-back-forward**—Hop forward, hop back, hop forward again, and shoot the ball.
- **Back-forward-back**—Hop backward, hop forward, hop back again, and shoot the ball.
- **Side-return-other side-return**—Hop to one side and back, then to the other side and back, and shoot the ball.

Ball position progression: Begin holding the ball directly at your release point (above shooting eye) and shooting the ball. You will not be able to perform this drill very far from the basket. Progress by lowering the initial ball position further (shoulder, then shot pocket), adding more arm motion, which will require greater arm and leg coordination.

Wrist Snap Drills: To Develop a Stronger Shooting Wrist

Wrist-Only Drill

Stand in front of the basket with your shooting arm fully extended and the ball laying in your shooting hand with your wrist cocked. Shoot the ball exclusively with the use of your wrist, making sure you get proper force and rotation (see Figure 1.28). Finish your shot by putting the two shooting fingers "into" the basket. Younger kids who are not able to get the ball over the rim can just shoot to themselves away from the basket following this procedure.

Figure 1.28 Wrist-only drill.

Wrist Flexibility Drill

Pull back your two shooting fingers with your nonshooting hand and let go, finishing the motion, snapping your wrist as you would during your follow-through (see Figure 1.29).

Figure 1.29 Wrist flexibility drill.

Shooting Alignment Drills

Line Shooting with a Partner Drill

Find a straight line on the basketball court (halfcourt or sideline, for example). One player stands in front of the other with the shooting foot placed on the shooting line. Shoot the ball back and forth to each other, letting it bounce on the line or as close as possible (see Figure 1.30). Focus on aligning your body parts with the line, ending the motion in balance on your toes, and holding your follow-through to develop a consistent and straight shot line.

Progression: Start with standard set shooting form (one-hand and/or your regular two-hand form), then progress into your jump shooting form.

Side of the Backboard Drill

Stand to the side of the backboard, 10'–12' away. Align your body and shoot the ball, aiming at a spot at least 10'–12' high on the side of the backboard (see Figure 1.31). A correct release will make the ball come back to you.

Progression: One-hand and/or two-hand form shooting, then progress to set shooting, and finally to jump shooting.

Figure 1.31 Side of the backboard drill.

Figure 1.30 Line shooting with a partner drill.

Wall Shooting Drill

Stand 10'–12' feet in front of a wall. Aim at a spot 10'–12' high on the wall. Shoot the ball—without throwing it—at the spot you are aiming for. Focus on proper alignment, follow-through, and finger control. A correct release will make the ball come back to you.

Progression: One-hand and/or two-hand form shooting, then progress to set shooting, and finally to jump shooting.

Elbow-In Drill

Hold the ball in your shooting pocket (stomach-chest area on strong side) with hands in shooting mode, elbow and forearm always at an approximately 90-degree angle (see Figure 1.32). Feel your elbow *in*, touching your hip. Like in your shooting motion, smoothly raise the ball up above your eye as if you were pump faking, and then lower it back down again, making sure your elbow just gently brushes your hip (no friction), therefore not "popping out." Repeat.

Figure 1.32 Elbow-in drill.

Drills To Develop Shooting Rhythm

Chair Shooting Drill 2

Sit on a chair, 10'–12' in front of the basket. Prepare your shot with correct hand placement and proper alignment in your shooting pocket, then smoothly rise to a standing position and release the ball in a fluid manner, ending the shot in balance on your toes while you follow through (see Figure 1.33). This method allows you to coordinate your leg motion with your arm motion, thus developing shooting rhythm. As a result, you will also improve your shooting range.

Progression: Set shooting to jump shooting; increase range.

Figure 1.33 Chair shooting drill 2.

Step-In Drill

Start with hands ready and knees flexed
on your reception. Catch the ball with
your shooting foot back and *step into* your
shot motion, getting maximum power and
momentum from your legs (see Figure 1.34).
Do not raise your hips, reload, or dip with the
ball. This method helps you generate good
shooting rhythm and also helps you shoot from
longer range.

Figure 1.34 Step-in drill.

Chapter 2

The Mental Side

While shooting technique is the most important aspect in shooting success, the mental side is another key factor. Great shooters have good mechanics and a high level of confidence, plus the ability to maintain concentration throughout an entire game. Even during stretches when they seem to be struggling to make shots, great shooters know how to bounce back to their standard levels of success.

CONCENTRATION

Concentration is as important in shooting as it is in basketball in general. You obviously cannot play, let alone make shots, without being focused on the game. In many ways, I believe that concentration is an overrated principle. If you do not have the self-discipline to focus on the game, then you should not even be on the team; evidently you don't care enough. Unless you have a major personal issue (health, family, academic, relationship problems, etc.), when you show up for the game or for a team practice, you must be focused. If you cannot concentrate while you are shooting the basketball then your problems go beyond putting the ball in the goal.

In my opinion, concentration is the ability to eliminate distraction and to control one's thoughts and emotions. Keep your head in the game!

Good practice habits and work ethic will enhance your concentration level.

Going through the process of mastering the skill of shooting, disciplining yourself, and training the right way will help you develop and/or improve your shooting concentration. As previously discussed, proper repetition of the correct shooting form will lead to an automatic shot execution. Relying on instincts and automatism, you will "think" less. Too much thinking can be a distraction and can hurt your concentration and your confidence. Good training habits will also improve your stamina, endurance, and general physical conditioning. To be a consistent shot maker, you rely on the consistency of your brain and your body. As you begin to feel fatigued, your concentration will also drop. Therefore, if both your body and your mind start to drift, so will your shot. In addition, your chances of injury will rise if you are not focused. Taking care of your body and staying in good physical shape will allow you to keep your concentration throughout the entire game.

CONFIDENCE

"Lack of confidence is born from a lack of preparation."
—Shannon Wilburn

You are more relaxed before an exam when you know that you have studied, not skipped any chapters, and understood what you have read. Same thing in shooting: if you have mastered the mechanics and consistently practiced, no doubt you will show up for the game confident in your abilities and optimistic about performing well.

Proper practice will lead to improvements and, eventually, successful results. This entire process will enhance your confidence, which will renew your dedication to more practice.

Confidence may develop gradually as you begin to see results in practice and in games. But it also may come all of a sudden, thanks to a positive experience—like making a game-winning shot or sinking two crucial free throws with the game on the line. Knowing you can do something should motivate you to work even harder.

Shooting should be the most fun part of the game. Nonetheless, many young players are hesitant to shoot because they are afraid they are going to miss and be criticized. The same thing can happen even to a veteran player at the end of a close game or during a playoff game as they begin to feel the pressure. As long as it is a good shot and within your range, you should take it. And a good shot, even if it doesn't go in, can lead to an offensive rebound and either a basket or a new possession.

Some players are anxious; some don't believe in themselves or their abilities. You can't be afraid of shooting the ball if it is a good shot opportunity. You can't make every shot in basketball. The best shooters in the game shoot about 50 percent from the field, so it is normal to miss half of your overall shots. The only way you can't miss a shot is by never attempting one. Remember that the basket is huge: the rim is almost two times the ball's diameter. This means that you have 4½ inches of margin for error all the way around. So even if your release is a bit off or slightly misdirected, it still has a pretty good chance of falling in.

Once again, your shooting mechanics should become an automatic motion. As you catch the ball, think "shot." Go straight up for your shot, without getting distracted by the crowd or your own thoughts. It should become routine. Thinking too much or overanalyzing each situation before you shoot will cause you to *hesitate* before you release the ball. This is the last thing you want to occur, because it will lead you to miss shots. High-level basketball is

> ## A Good Follow-Through is the Sign of a Confident Shooter!
>
> Confident shooters are so focused on the rim that they hold their follow-through an extra second or two, even when the ball has already gone through the rim.

played on instincts. If you think too much, you will be hesitant and react too slowly.

You must have a positive mindset when you are on the floor and every time you are about to shoot. Believe in all the work you put in. Know that you can and will make the shot. Never think "I hope I don't miss this one," or "I can't do this," but instead, "I'm going to make the next one." Most great shooters talk to themselves and use reinforcement words like *all net*, *boom*, *swish*, *money*, etc. It's obviously very subjective.

Don't overanalyze every shot unless you are learning how to shoot or making some form adjustments during your mechanics training phase. During repetitions, competitive training, and especially games, you must be so focused that you never stop and dwell on a missed shot. It's important to learn how to instantly "analyze, correct, and forget" a mistake. Remember the shots that feel good. Forget the misses, but learn from them. Control your emotions, think positively, and stay focused. Don't start cussing, shaking your head, or kicking the ball after a miss; instead, bounce right back for your next shot.

Shooter's Attitude

Confident shooters develop an *attitude* where they are so determined and sure of their ability to shoot the ball successfully that they think they can make every shot. This doesn't mean that they jack up a shot every time they catch the ball or talk trash to opponents, but they do create their own mindset, talking to

Shooting **TIP**

"When it comes to taking clutch shots, I'm at ease mentally whether the shot is in the first quarter or the fourth quarter. I don't put any extra pressure on myself and I don't worry about the outcome of the shot."
—**Chauncey Billups**

Chauncey Billups isn't nicknamed "Mr. Big Shot" for nothing! His confidence, concentration, and leadership make him one of the top clutch shooters in the game. (Photo by Garrett W. Ellwood/NBAE via Getty Images)

Shooting **TIP**

"I want to help my team win so badly that I am willing to take the responsibility of a big shot, well aware of the consequences whether I make it or not."

—Derek Fisher

themselves, psyching themselves up, keeping their concentration and confidence levels high. They go to the free throw line and saying to themselves, "Two more for me." This is part of developing the "killer instinct" that separates the best from the rest. Confident shooters are eager to take big shots and don't lose confidence after a couple missed shots or a poor shooting night. They might miss a shot, but still believe they will make the next one.

The more shots you make, the more confident you get! There is a thin line between confident and cocky, so don't let your overconfidence lead you to presumption, which at some point will backfire as you might think you don't need to train anymore. Great shooters constantly renew their confidence through good practice habits and repetition, challenging themselves every day.

MENTAL VISUALIZATION

Consistent training and repetition will instill muscle memory for an automatic shot. But you can reinforce this with *mental training*. In fact, repeating the correct shooting mechanics in your mind will also contribute to improving the automatism of your shot motion. Mental

Figure 2.1 Mental visualization.

practice—imagining a smooth shooting action and a clear mental picture of the ball going through the goal—will help your shot become more automatic, help you develop a better shooting rhythm, enhance your concentration, and instill confidence thanks to the positive image (see Figure 2.1).

This entire mental visualization procedure will make you feel good about your shot, your form, and yourself. Confident shooters expect to make every shot as they always have a perfect image of a successful shot in their minds. They know what a good shot looks like and feels like. They know when the ball will drop through the basket even before it actually does. Concentration, confidence, and positive mental imagery work closely together, complementing one another and sending positive energy throughout the body during the shot motion.

SHOOTING SLUMPS

It is common even for high-level players to hit a so-called "shooting slump" at some point during the season where the ball just won't go in. This could be caused by lack of confidence, a reduced role on the team, being out of shape, an injury, shot selection, or just being fatigued because of the stress and length of the basketball season. The more they shoot and miss, the more frustrated they might become, leading to a total loss of confidence in their shooting abilities and overall game. Whatever the cause, shooting slumps are usually *mental*. While it is only human to run into this kind of problem, good shooters will overcome it through patience and proper practice as they regain their confidence.

Getting Out of a Shooting Slump

Whether you are missing shots because of a mechanical problem in your form or because of a concentration and/or confidence issue, the best way of getting out of a shooting slump is to give yourself a mechanics "review course." Go back to the shooting basics in a calm practice environment, such as in a gym you are familiar with and feel comfortable in. Find quality time alone or with a good partner, or better yet with your coach. Perform classic drills that you practiced when you began learning how to shoot. Practice one-hand shooting to make sure your shooting hand is holding the ball correctly and giving the right direction (see Figure 2.2); two hand form shooting, finding your rhythm and stroke, slowly working your way farther away from the hoop; and free throws. This

Figure 2.2 One-hand shooting.

Shooting **TIP**

"If you fall into a little slump or feel something wrong in your shot, don't overreact. You don't need to shoot 1,000 shots. Go back to the basics, then work yourself up."
—Glen Rice

method will allow you to refresh your basic shooting technique step by step and to regain your confidence. Then begin getting your legs back into your shot—from all positions—find your range, and progress to your usual "game speed" shots.

Also, during the time you are not feeling good about your shot and feel somewhat insecure shooting the ball, it's a good idea to begin games by letting the game come to you: not forcing shots, but perhaps waiting for a good open shot opportunity. Try attacking the basket, drawing a foul, and maybe hitting a couple free throws. Converting a few foul shots at the beginning of a game is definitely a good way of getting your groove back.

Coming Back From an Injury or Time Off

"My shot doesn't feel right." You've either said it or heard it countless times. Most of the time this happens when you are returning to the court after time off from playing: after the season, a vacation, or an injury. Or you might have a nagging injury that bothers you and are struggling to find your rhythm and feel uncomfortable shooting the ball. It could be that your body is not in the best shape and needs time to re-adapt to the practice stress and physical and athletic demands of playing basketball. A little pain or instability in your back, knee, ankle, elbow, wrist, etc., could be

more of the problem than your actual shooting form. Don't let this affect your mental approach and confidence in your shooting technique. Have patience, whether getting into your best shape or healing from the injury, and your shot will start feeling good again.

So, as in dealing with shooting slumps, the best "cure" is going back to practicing the basics: review your basic mechanics with close-range form shooting, and avoid long-range shots and high-energy gamelike intensity shooting until your body and shot tell you that you are ready. This way you will not compensate for any lack of strength/stability or stamina in your body. Since the ball might feel somewhat like a "foreign object," it is a good idea to begin your workouts with some ball-handling drills to regain your feel for the ball first (see Figure 2.3). Consequently your feel for the basket will also improve.

Remember: stay in shape and take care of your body!

Figure 2.3 Ball-handling drills.

Shooting **TIP**

"If I'm not 100 percent physically, I can feel it in my shot."
—Chauncey Billups

"Do This, Do That"

When you are not making shots, everyone will try to give you advice and suggestions. You'll hear countless different concepts, methods, and strategies from teammates, coaches, family, friends…and even fans! The result is that you will feel more pressure and end up being totally confused. Listen to the *one* basketball person you trust and believe in *your* mechanics practicing. As you begin to see the ball go in again, your confidence and comfort level will rise. Move back one step at a time until you are hitting shots consistently from your usual shooting range.

Shot Selection

Most great shooters don't get into an actual slump. However, their shot selection might become questionable and their shooting percentage could drop. Tight defenses, double teaming, and poor team ball circulation might cause a player to force shots or have to throw up a bad shot as the possession clock runs out. Missed (bad) shots will lead to frustration and then lead to stubbornness, as you might force more poor shots. I wouldn't call this a shooting slump because it sounds more like a team problem, a selfishness matter, or a shot concept issue that your coach must address. But if your frustrations cause you to change your shooting mechanics or you begin feeling something different in your form, you should go back to the basics.

Chapter 3

The Free Throw

Why did I decide to dedicate an entire section to free throw shooting? Because I consider the free throw the *mother* of all shots—both the ultimate *mechanical* shot and the ultimate *mental* shot.

Everything we have addressed so far in the shooting mechanics and the mental side sections can be put together at the foul line: from feet and hands to rhythm and confidence.

I don't think coaches, at any level, stress to their players the importance of free throw shooting. I have been a free throw fanatic ever since I was a young player. Making a big deal about free throws makes players realize how important they are to the game—not only because better free throw shooting leads to improvements in a player's shooting technique, but also because free throws often decide a game's outcome!

No matter how advanced a player or shooter you are, when you are struggling with your shot or in a so-called shooting slump, you should go back and review your basic mechanics and checkpoints. There is no better place to do this than the free throw line because it allows you to relax, focus, analyze, correct, and regain your normal shooting confidence from an appropriate range. Afterward, you will progress into your game shots and long-range shots.

You must incorporate free throw shooting in every practice or individual workout. Many teams and players just shoot free throws at the end of practice or during a water break. This is not enough and not gamelike. You must shoot several free throw sets (two shots at a time) during the actual practice to re-create game fatigue and stress. Shooting two free throws is also a great way to catch your breath between drills, without stopping, during an individual training session. Coaches must make each player accountable.

Steve Nash has shot more than 90 percent at the foul line throughout his incredible career. (Photo by Tim Heitman/ NBAE via Getty Images)

A UNIQUE SITUATION

Free throw shooting is a big part of the game of basketball, but it is a different shot because its setting occurs in a unique situation. It's a different, special, unusual, but ideal situation to be able to make an uncontested shot with enough time to prepare for it—no defender, no running, no cutting, no catching, no hurry… and no excuses! You can use all of these positive factors to work in your favor or let

Making Every Free Throw

It's impossible to make every shot in basketball. There are just too many variables and factors. Confident shooters should believe that they can, but it is impossible.

Crazy or not, when it comes to free throw shooting, I believe that a player who has mastered good mechanics and has developed great concentration and confidence through constant practice can make nearly every shot. Maybe not if you are shooting 1,000 shots at once, but if you have two shots at a time, I believe that you can reach near perfection.

Shooting TIP

"The free throw is a mental shot for most players. The 90-percent foul shooters put no pressure on themselves; it's just automatic routine. The poor ones feel all eyes on them and overthink, worried about the outcome of the shot."
—Glen Rice

them work against you. It all depends on your level of confidence…or anxiety.

What I like about free throw shooting is that a free throw is a fair shot: everyone is the same at the foul line. It doesn't matter how tall, strong, big, old, or talented you are. Whether male or female, amateur or pro, no one has an advantage over another, and the shot's outcome depends only on *you*.

Why is the Free Throw Such a Complicated Shot?

The free throw really is not complicated, but many players allow themselves to believe that it is a difficult shot, thus letting an advantageous setting work against them.

The foul shot setting is different from any game situation, where your shooting relies more on instincts because you have to catch and shoot as quickly as possible. There is very little thinking involved: you're open, you shoot! In fact, there have been many examples of successful perimeter shooters who were just mediocre foul shooters.

At the free throw line you have a large amount of time between the whistle blow and the actual release of the shot. Throw in a timeout perhaps, especially at the end of a game, and by this time your thoughts might have gotten the best of you and the amount

of pressure could have doubled in your mind. This anxiety and overthinking is what you want to avoid. The only way to do so is by eliminating negative thoughts and distractions and believing in the hours of practice you have put in to develop your good shooting form, confident attitude, and automatic free throw routine.

Confidence Might Develop From a Successful Experience

My biggest basketball nightmare as a kid was having to shoot two free throws to win the game. I was terrified at the idea of my teammates and all of the parents blaming me for the team losing. My thoughts were more along the lines of, "I don't want the team to lose because of me," than, "I want to win a game for us." Funny how when I was 17 years old this scenario presented itself. With my team down by one point with only a few seconds left, I drew a foul and had two free throws. I was nervous, but on the other hand knew I was a pretty good foul shooter. I made both and we won. The relief was huge, not only for winning that particular game and not taking any blame, but also I just felt I got it out of my system. After that, I become much more confident from the free throw line, eager to try to put myself in that same situation again.

FIVE REASONS TO PRACTICE YOUR FREE THROWS

1. Best Place to Learn Your Mechanics and Practice Them

Free throw shooting is the best setting and the proper distance to practice your form, to learn to analyze your own shot, and to make mechanical adjustments (see Figure 3.1). You don't have a defender to disrupt your motion and you have time to prepare for the execution.

2. Develops Confidence

The free throw line is where shooting confidence develops. Repetitive foul shooting will instill muscle memory and make your shot automatic. You will master a routine where every time you walk up to the free throw line, you will be so confident that you will expect to make every shot. This confidence will transfer to your jump shooting and to the rest of your game, as you will even be more aggressive driving to the basket. You will want to draw fouls, knowing that you will score the two foul shots.

3. Free Throws Win Games

When a game is lost by three points or less I always look at the free throws missed. Let's say your team shot 70 percent at the foul line, your opponents shot 85 percent, and you lost by just two points...what do you think? It's amazing how a team can outplay an opponent, but still lose the game because of a superficial approach at the foul line. Free throws make up about 25 percent of the total points in an average basketball game. Do you dedicate 25 percent of your practice or workout to shooting foul shots? Probably not. If you cannot find the time for more free throw shooting during your usual team practice, you must find some quality time to do so before or after.

4. A Good Free Throw Shooter Will Get Quality Playing Time

Being a good free throw shooter will get you more minutes on the floor and permit you to be on the court at the end of big games. If you are a poor foul shooter you will probably be on the bench at the end of games; and if you are on the court, your teammates will be reluctant to pass you the ball just in case you do get fouled.

5. You Can *Capitalize* At the Free Throw Line

You have the opportunity to score more points at the line. Even on a bad shooting night, you can still help your team win by simply hitting your free throws. Also, scoring two free throws early in a game will

Figure 3.1 Free throw practice.

help you find your groove without having to rush shots. Good one-on-one scorers will drive a lot, draw contact, get fouled, and often find themselves at the free throw line. If they are not high percentage free throw shooters, they become liabilities for their teams.

DEVELOPING A ROUTINE

Constant repetition at the free throw line will lead to developing a routine. Adopting a free throw routine that proves to work for you can help you relax and will enhance your concentration, confidence, and automatism of the motion—all keys to making a higher percentage of shots.

Your routine should always be exactly the same and not rushed. The entire ritual and motion should be so automatic that you are relying more on muscle memory than actually thinking about the shot.

The routine will make you focus on each of its steps rather than the outcome of the shot and the score of the game. In addition, it takes your eyes off the target for a moment, alleviating much of the pressure in your mind. You should never stare at the rim too long to try to focus better. That doesn't work and may actually make you more nervous. Focus on the routine's steps to relax while picturing a perfect shot, with the ball right above the goal about to swish through the net, in your mind.

All great free throw shooters have their own rituals at the foul line. All routines are different as they are personal, so don't try to imitate somebody else's. Find what works for you. Whether it's one dribble or three, two big breaths, a mechanical reminder (like "elbow in"), or a special word you say to yourself, develop *your* routine. Nothing fancy, flashy, or overly creative. Keep it simple, consistent, and efficient, and make sure it makes you feel as comfortable and confident as possible when

Tall Players: Find Your Rhythm!

Tall players are usually strong enough not to need much leg power for their shots. Having longer limbs, big players need to control excess motion.

But without any knee bending it's hard to find proper rhythm in free throw shooting. In fact, most centers' flaws at the foul line have to do with their stiffness and choppy rhythm.

Just a little knee flexion can help generate proper rhythm into the shot. While striving for economy of motion is correct, giving up shooting rhythm will hurt your free throw technique.

you step to the line. You have 10 seconds to prepare your feet and hands, focus, aim, and release the ball. Take your time, you are in no hurry. Your routine should take six to eight seconds for its execution.

Let your routine guide you through each free throw. Automatic motion every time!

Recommended Guidelines and Checkpoints for Your Routine

Simple, consistent, efficient, and automatic—that's what you are looking for! While you must develop your own personal free throw routine, you should follow certain guidelines. These are the main checkpoints I recommend.

- Position your shooting toe so it is aligned with the middle of the basket (most hardwood floors have a nail exactly in the middle of the foul line). Your back foot's toe is even with the instep of your lead foot (see Figure 3.2). Position yourself with 10 toes pointing to the basket, feet shoulder-width apart. Find good balance. Locate the rim and double-check your alignment with the basket, as it will determine your shot line.
- Flex your knees, hips, and ankles right away; take one to three dribbles; and *relax* (see Figure 3.3). Most players take their dribbles

Figure 3.2 Shooting toe.

Figure 3.3 Flex your knees, hips, and ankles.

before they bend their legs, but I prefer you to be already down, so that you are already "loaded" and the rim level is always the same to your eyes. Do not focus on the rim yet.

- Position the ball in your hands. Knees stay flexed as you feel the ball, adjusting your fingers and grip on it. Look for the inflation valve on the middle of the ball and place your two shooting fingers (index and middle) in the seam right above. Now the valve is in between your shooting fork, so you know the fingers are in the middle of ball. Wrist is cocked and the ball is in your shooting pocket (the strong side of your stomach-chest area below the shoulder).

- Take a deep breath to relax and begin to focus on the rim: visualize the ball dropping straight down the middle of the basket with a perfect swish. Repeat your reinforcement words to yourself. Don't take your eyes off the rim for the rest of the free throw motion.

- Begin the extension sequence now. Avoid any hesitation from this point on. Raise the ball above your shooting eye (strong side of the forehead area) to your release point, as your legs are also beginning to extend. Use an upward and forward arm extension (ankles give final push at this time), and snap your wrist, thrusting the ball with a confident follow-through. Freeze your follow-through two seconds with your fingers down, with your eyes still on the rim, balancing your body on your toes. You should realize right away just by "feel" if the ball was released properly, so if you have to, you will make a little adjustment on the following shot.

Pointers on Free Throw Shooting

- Shooting toe lined up with the middle of the rim. This determines your shot line.
- Position your shooting fingers (shooting fork) in the seam of the ball and straddle

its inflation valve. This will allow a better backspin as you release the ball and ensures that your two shooting fingers are centered in the middle of the ball.

- Don't rush: you have 10 seconds.
- Don't break your rhythm. Everything goes up together from a proper shooting pocket position. Avoid any hesitation and/or hitch.
- Hold your follow-through, while extending your feet.
- Without crossing the line, balance your body on your toes as you hold the follow-through. Head, chest, and shoulders should end slightly forward from your initial position. If you fall back on your heels, your shoulders will also fall back, causing negative motion.
- Let your routine guide you through each free throw: automatic motion every time.
- Don't change your routine every time you miss a free throw.
- Don't stare at the rim through the entire routine.
- Long is better than short. Short means *not* confident or is a sign of indecision or tension somewhere. A good follow-through means you are confident!
- Usually you have two free throws. Focus on one shot at a time. Even while practicing, don't think about making 100 in a row or about the total number or goal you're trying to reach. One shot at a time!
- Your first shot is the most important mentally. You can always make an adjustment on the second attempt. A missed second shot may give your team an offensive rebound opportunity.
- Readjust your feet after every two free throws if you are shooting a large number of free throws at once.
- You should *never* miss two free throws in a row. And most of all you should never miss two shots in the same manner. It should be much harder to miss two than to make two in a row.

Shooting TIP

"I've used the same free throw routine since I was 17 years old. Find something that works for you and stick with it."
—**Chauncey Billups**

- Keep it realistic: two shots at a time (but sometimes one free throw and three free throws).
- I do not believe in practicing free throws with your eyes closed. I understand the reason and the goal, but since you don't shoot blindfolded in real games, why would you train that way?

FREE THROW DRILLS AND GAMES

You can perform these drills/games by yourself, challenging a partner, or in a small group of players.

Swish Drill

This drill forces you to become a total perfectionist at the foul line because you are not only trying to convert the shots, but also wanting them to fall straight down the middle of the basket without hitting either the rim or the backboard. And even though you might not be reaching the drill's goal initially, you still will be improving your overall free throw mechanics, routine, confidence, and percentage. Each swish (only net) is worth +1 point, each miss counts as -1 (thus setting you back), and each made shot that is not a swish (touches the rim/backboard before falling in) is worth zero points.

Beginners: goal is to reach +5 points.
Advanced: goal is to reach +10 points.

Note: *It is possible to shoot 100 percent and never reach the goal of the drill!*

Plus/Minus Games

This game forces you to compete against yourself. Each time you score a basket you get one point, but each time you miss a basket you lose one point. Play games up to +10 or +20 points, depending on your level.

Beginner Level: +1 point each made shot, -1 point each missed shot.

Intermediate Level: +1 point each made shot, -2 points each missed shot.

Advanced Level: +1 point each made shot, -3 points each missed shot.

Pro Level: +1 point each made shot, -5 points each missed shot.

Note: *You can perform this drill from any spot on the floor. You can stay in one spot throughout the game or you can change spots on each shot. Use your creativity, just make sure they are your game spots within your shooting range.*

Challenging a Partner

Competing with a partner can raise the level of the workout and can help you avoid boredom. Some days you might have to push a friend; other days your friend will be the one to carry you if you're fatigued. You can work on a "mutual goal," which helps build teamwork. For example, together you must score at least 18 out of 20 shots or you can challenge each other in competitive games, shooting 10, 20, 30, or 50 shots each. Whoever scores the most baskets out of the number of attempts wins. If you end in a tie, continue until somebody misses; this will increase the level of pressure on each shot. However you play, focus mainly on sets of two shots at a time each. You should also play occasional games with sets of three shots each (as if you were fouled on a three-point shot), and also one shot each (as if it was a technical foul or a "and one" shot after being fouled on a made basket). Variations are welcome as long as you keep the challenge games realistic and competitive.

Chapter 4

Game Situations

COURT AWARENESS AND SPACING PRINCIPLES

Before discussing game situations and factors regarding the act of shooting the basketball, it's important to address some basic principles to facilitate recognizing where and when there is a good shot opportunity, and where to move in order to find one.

Basketball is a game of spacing and angles. Knowing your court geography and having good court awareness means being familiar with the size of the floor and identifying the best areas of operation, shooting spots, and angles for perimeter and inside players. You must know, see, and feel the basketball court—always remaining aware of your position and those of your teammates. Too many times I see players stepping out of bounds, receiving the ball too low on the block or behind the backboard, standing in the same spot as a teammate, ending up underneath the rim, dribbling into congested areas, etc. The bottom line is they don't have good court sense.

Proper spacing is crucial for good ball movement, efficient team play, and good shot selection. The offense's goal is not to allow one defender to cover two players. If players maintain a distance of 15'–18' from each other, they will not overcrowd areas of the floor and will have their own room to operate.

Overdribbling and standing still will lead to static offensive play that will kill

The Triangle Offense

Working for the Lakers and being around the Triangle Offense for many years, it has been fascinating to watch how coaches Phil Jackson and Tex Winter would introduce the offense to new players in training camp. Right from the start, they focus on basics such as footwork techniques, positions on the floor, and spacing principles.

"From wherever I catch the ball on the court, I know where the basket is and know how much strength I will need to put into the shot."
—Chuck Person

Chuck Person, known as the Rifleman, shows his soft touch.
(Tim de Frisco/Allsport)

ball movement and allow the defense to adapt or rest. Good court awareness, correct spacing and timing, and execution of the fundamental skills—driving, cutting, passing, and catching—will open up great scoring opportunities for the offense: one-on-one situations and open shots.

PLAYING WITHOUT THE BALL: GETTING OPEN FOR RECEPTION

Becoming a good shooter begins with proper mechanics and a high level of confidence. But these two qualities alone are not going to lead to success in real games. You would be a very limited player, despite perhaps being a dead-eye shooter. Your ability to get open in a good spot on the court in position to quickly execute your shot is fundamentally important to becoming a good shooter and a solid one-on-one threat.

Getting open to receive the ball means moving and cutting without the ball and trying to create a time and/or space lead over your defender. Reception must occur in a spot on the court that doesn't compromise your teammates' spacing and within your shooting range, from where you can shoot, pass, or dribble.

The best players at playing without the ball are *not* necessarily the quickest ones.

Shooting TIP

"Playing without the ball is a lost art. It's one of the most important but overlooked aspects in shooting. Most defenders aren't willing to chase players around the court. Even an average shooter can become a threat by playing well without the ball."

—Glen Rice

But they have great levels of stamina and endurance, know how to change pace, set up their defenders, and use their own bodies and others' bodies (screens or creating contact with opponent) efficiently. Larry Bird is a great example of a player with limited speed, but with an incredible ability to move without the ball in order to free himself. Understanding angles and spacing principles is very important.

You might move to get open on your own or with help from your teammates. Following are some basic techniques for both inside and perimeter players to create a lead on the defender without the help of a screen to receive the ball in shooting position in the wing area.

Shooting TIP

"Moving without the ball is not about being fast. Setting up your defender with a quick change of speed from the regular rhythm of the game is what gets you open."

—Kiki Vandeweghe

Footwork

Working with players of all ages from youth to the NBA, I am shocked with the consistently poor level of footwork. Whether it's the angle of the cut, the change of pace, or just the planting of the foot, I have come to realize that even the average pro player doesn't know how to execute a proper V cut.

Players must learn how to perform the very basic but fundamental footwork skills if they want to learn how to get open.

Four Techniques

While performing these techniques, focus on using the ball of your foot—not the entire foot—as you push off changing direction. This will allow you to move quicker and more explosively.

V Cut—Take your defender one way at a slow speed. Plant your foot and change your speed and direction, creating a "V" to open up for reception (see Figure 4.1). Square up to the basket.

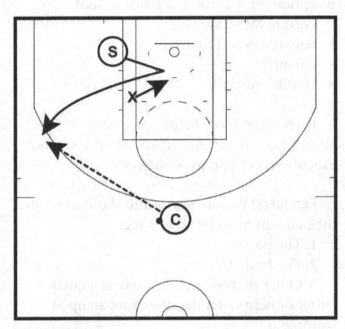

Figure 4.1 V cut.

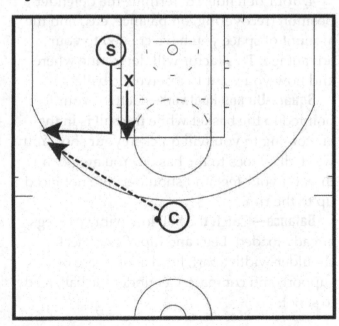

Figure 4.2 L cut.

L Cut—Take your defender up the lane line and cut the defender off with your inside leg and inside arm/shoulder. Now push off your inside foot at a 90-degree angle (L-shape cut) with a change of speed for reception (see Figure 4.2). Square up to the basket.

Reverse—Your defender denies your reception on the wing. Take the defender "in" toward the paint, and then plant your foot (closest one to the passer) between the defender's legs and reverse pivot, "sealing" the defender on your back. Pop back out with a change of speed for reception in the wing area; square up to the basket (see Figure 4.3).

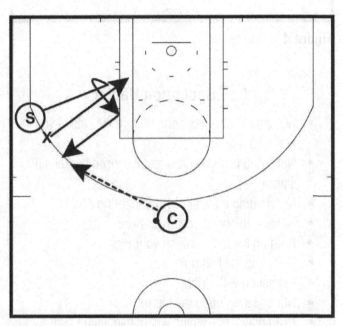

Figure 4.3 Reverse.

Circle—Your defender plays you tight, face to face, not allowing you to cut off the defender. Fake one step out to the wing with your outside foot, then quickly move it back and around, circling the defender. You will end up in front of the defender now, similar to a "boxing out" position (see Figure 4.4). Break out to the wing with a change of speed for reception; square up to the basket.

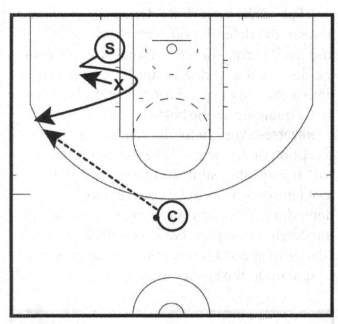

Figure 4.4 Circle.

Bad Reception Habits

- Reception out of your shooting range, where you are not a threat
- Not being in a good low and balanced basketball stance
- Not holding the ball in your shooting pocket
- Holding the ball above your head
- Holding the ball between your legs
- Dribbling the ball right away
- Retreating with dribble
- Not squaring up to the basket
- Head down, not seeing what's happening on the court

RECEPTION

Good reception starts with good movement without the ball in order to create a lead, which is a small time and/or space advantage over your defender that allows you to catch in the best position and condition possible to be able to shoot, pass, or dribble.

Your ultimate goal is to be able to catch a pass in an opportune position and make a good shot. Good movement without the ball

Get all your work done before you receive the ball!

leads to an opening, which leads to a good reception that allows you to get your shot off comfortably. Remember that gaining a one-second or a 2' advantage on your defender is huge in the game of basketball.

There are four key components of good reception for a quick and efficient shot:
- Peripheral vision
- Square-up and footwork
- Balance
- Hands "ready"

Each component helps you create an additional advantage and speed up your shot execution. Let's analyze each one:

Peripheral Vision—As you're about to receive the ball you must be able to see:
1. The passer
2. The basket
3. Other players, in case there is a quick cutter or help-defender, therefore an open teammate
4. Your defender: determine the defender's position (recovering, off balance, etc.) and the amount of space you have created to your advantage. This factor will determine where and how you want to receive the ball.

Square-Up and Footwork—Getting your feet pointed to the basket while the ball is in the air coming to you will quicken your shot. You want all 10 toes to the basket. You are not a threat if your feet and shoulders are not faced up to the rim.

Balance—Catch the ball low with your legs already loaded. Legs and hips flexed, feet shoulder-width apart, head above base of support, and compact. Get under the ball, ready to shoot.

Show Your Palms!

I have a rule during my shooting stations at basketball camps: don't pass the ball to players who don't show their palms. It means they don't want the ball.

Hands Ready—Give a good target and show where you want the ball (shot pocket area). Hands above elbows, showing palms (see Figure 4.5). Wrist should already be cocked when possible. If you are open, a good passer will throw the pass right in front of you, so you are ready to shoot. Don't reach for the ball unless the pass is way off or the defense is very tight.

Figure 4.5 Hands ready.

Rip Hamilton, one of the best players in the NBA at moving without the ball, shows how to catch a pass on the move. (Photo by Gregory Shamus/NBAE via Getty Images)

SHOOTING FOOTWORK

Good footwork is the foundation to performing all of the game's offensive and defensive fundamentals with proper balance and at the right speed, from moving without the ball to rebounding, and from defending to shooting. Earlier you learned how the first part of your shot begins with the feet. Proper footwork is one of the key factors in catching and shooting, and mastering one-on-one moves to the basket.

Shooting footwork is one of the most complex subjects in basketball fundamentals. Coaches have different philosophies and methods of teaching, and all players have their own interpretations because of their size, coordination, balance, and physical and athletic abilities. A good instructor should show young players all of the different methods, explain their advantages, make the kids experiment with all footwork techniques, and teach them how to use them in each particular game situation.

Just like you work on your ball handling with both hands, you must train your feet to be able to jump, jab, V cut, slide, and pivot equally well with either foot. This will give you more offensive options, allow you to be able to move in any direction with balance and speed, and help you avoid traveling calls. After all, you play the entire game with your feet, and only parts of it with your hands. Players must find footwork that works best, allowing the best possible balance, comfort, and quickness to shoot the ball properly. Different situations

Shooting TIP

"My footwork is very important to me. You need strong legs and good balance to be able to get a good shot off."

—Rudy Fernandez

command different footwork, depending on your defender and possibly your cutting angle or position on the floor.

After you've determined which footwork works best for you, allowing you the best balance and most quickness to eventually get your shot off (reception, catch and shoot, and off the dribble) try to keep it consistent. Then your shot will also become more consistent.

Footwork Options

Whether you are receiving the ball or pulling up for your shot off the dribble, there are two basic footwork techniques: the 1-2 Stop and the Jump Stop. Both have advantages and disadvantages. Therefore I feel that all players, especially at a young age, should practice both methods. Then, depending on their feel, balance, size, quickness, and coordination, they will figure out which works better for them. In any case, footwork may vary according to the situation, the defender's position, and the player's different angles on the floor.

Both methods must be performed catching the ball (off the pass or off the dribble), with your hands ready, body low, and knees and hips flexed, allowing the best balance possible. Bring the ball into your shot pocket as quickly as possible and go straight up for the shot.

1-2 Stop

In the scoring area, the 1-2 is usually performed using an inside pivot, the foot closest to the basket. This is the most-used method of

Shooting TIP

"Good footwork comes from both physical and mental balance."

—Kiki Vandeweghe

Shooting **TIP**

"The 1-2 stop is the quickest and most efficient footwork for shooting the ball."

—Jerry West

stopping to receive the ball and shooting off the dribble, and in most cases the most efficient because it is quicker and offers better protection. Planting your first foot, with a heel-to-toe rolling motion, you break your momentum as the second foot provides balance and squares up the rest of your body to the goal (see Figure 4.6). Depending on your angle, you might need to rotate your ankle to point it to the rim. Most of your weight is on your pivot foot, while only the ball of your "gathering" foot touches the ground as it gives the initial vertical push to go up for the shot. During the 1-2, your feet stay close to the ground, making it quicker than the jump stop, where you lose time hopping in the air, allowing your defender to recover.

A modern-day athlete who played in the '60s and early '70s, and one of the game's most fundamentally sound players ever, Jerry West excelled in shooting off the dribble. (Photo by Dick Raphael/NBAE via Getty Images)

Figure 4.6 1-2 stop.

The 1-2 Stop can be performed using either a front pivot or a reverse pivot:

1. Front Pivot—This is the most-used method to catch the ball and face the basket, and to actually shoot the ball. You should establish your inside foot as your pivot and turn your body forward toward the basket (see Figure 4.7). This is also the technique you use while shooting off the dribble.

2. Reverse Pivot—When performing the front pivot, you are moving toward the basket, shortening the distance from the goal. In contrast, a reverse pivot involves negative motion, as you are moving away from the goal, thus increasing the distance from the rim (see Figure 4.8). There is also less protection, as you are opening up (outside pivot foot) and exposing the ball to the defense. Although this method

Figure 4.7 Front pivot.

Figure 4.8 Reverse pivot.

is often used in other circumstances (defense, rebounding, rolling after setting a screen, etc.), it is used less than the front pivot for catching and shooting the ball. However, in some situations and positions, depending on the angle of your cut and reception, and also on the way your defender is playing you, it can be very beneficial. For example, you might use it to face up after using an L cut out to the wing or you might prefer using it to create space between you and an aggressive opponent. This is a very efficient footwork technique for post-up players who might have gotten pushed off the low-post block. Give a target with your outside hand and as you catch the pass, reverse pivot on your outside foot (farthest from the basket), and either shoot the jump shot (the Sikma Move, as Jack Sikma was a master at this technique) or pump fake, crossover, and attack the middle of the paint. Mastering both 1-2 footwork techniques in the low post and high post can give a post-up player a variety of opportunities to score.

Jump Stop

This technique is less used than the 1-2 stop because only certain players with exceptionally

Shooting **TIP**

"Establishing position with a two-foot jump stop in the low post allows you to have options for any way the defender is playing you."
—**Vlade Divac**

strong legs and great balance use it efficiently. You jump off one foot, usually the inside foot, and land on both feet simultaneously (see Figure 4.9). On your reception, this allows you to jump behind the ball for a quick square up and to choose your pivot foot. It is best to use this technique when you are moving straight toward the basket. A player can use the jump stop in the scoring area to gain additional separation off the dribble, using a forward "hop" to beat and cut off the defender. In this situation, a two-foot jump stop might offer better body control and more stability in the air to absorb contact while shooting. The downside

Figure 4.9 Jump stop.

of the jump stop, especially off the dribble, is that there is less protection and that it's slower than the 1-2 because that "hop" needs more loading time and more air time and might allow your defender to recover. Try keeping your feet closest to the floor, in order to reduce this air time. Moving at your highest speed, the jump stop offers less control than the 1-2 stop, where you can "brake" with your pivot foot, slowing yourself down. For low-post players, the jump stop is the best way to establish position with their backs to the basket or to score with a power move.

Incorporating both the 1-2 stop, with front and reverse pivots, and the jump stop in your practice drills will surely improve your overall footwork, balance, and body control and help you become a better shooter and a more fundamentally sound basketball player.

THREE SITUATIONS = THREE RECEPTIONS

These are the most common game situations for shooting:
1. **Spotting Up** (open to shoot)
2. **In Motion** (after creating a lead)
3. **Aggressive Defense** (no lead)

1. Spotting Up—This occurs when you are open without having to move or cut and only have to catch the pass and comfortably shoot. Feet should never be planted, but always live and ready to move. A good passer will throw a proper pass so that you can catch it in front of your body. You may use a 1-2, stepping in as you catch and square up, or a little hop. This hop is different than the jump stop. You do land on both feet simultaneously, but you take out the jump and the airtime. As you catch the pass, you *drop* into your basketball

Your Dominant Foot

Just as we all have a dominant hand, we also have a dominant foot. Although practice aims to improve our weak hand and weak foot, we will always be more comfortable with the dominant ones.

If you are right-handed, you are probably also right-footed, but a better leaper off your left leg; vice versa if you're left-handed.

Most players will naturally try to make their nonshooting foot their pivot as they get into their triple threat stance. You are better coordinated with your dominant foot, you can jab better, and you can step into the shot more naturally to provide the necessary force and rhythm.

stance and go up for the shot. If a pass is slightly off, jump behind the ball for a quicker release instead of reaching for the ball.

2. In Motion—This is when you have created a lead on your defender either on your own or with the help of a screen. With your peripheral vision you can see how much space you have gained and you know you can get the shot off. Catch the ball whenever possible with an inside pivot, square up, and shoot. If your defender is recovering, use a pump fake and beat the defender off the dribble.

3. Aggressive Defense—This can be either a static or a dynamic situation. Your defender is playing you tight; you have not created an opening. You know you can't get your feet pointed at the basket on your reception and are forced to reach for the ball away from your defender. Use your outside hand as a target, away from the defender, and go meet the ball. Establish an *inside pivot* for protection, with shoulders perpendicular to your defender's chest, and then turn (a two-count motion) to face the basket, driving your opponent back with an aggressive jab step. Now you are squared to the basket and you are a threat. If your defender's hands are low, shoot. If your defender is in correct position you will rely on your Triple Threat moves (drive or pull-up jump shot) or make a good pass to a teammate in better position. If your defender overplays as you catch the pass, quickly use either a sweep-through crossover step or a reverse step and go to the basket (See Figure 4.10).

Figure 4.10 If your defender overplays as you catch the pass, react quickly with either a sweep-through crossover step or a reverse step directly to the basket.

Glen Rice shows how an inside pivot provides the best protection against an aggressive defender. (Jonathan Ferrey/Getty Images)

SHOT FAKES

Shot fakes must be believable to be effective. You must sell your jump shot well to really trick your defender. Also, the fake must be executed at the right speed: neither too quick nor too slow. Your goal is to make your defender react, but if the fake is just too quick, the defender won't even have time to see it and will stay put. If it is too slow, your opponent will have no problem adjusting to your inefficient move. Fake in a believable manner: "selling" with your true shot technique, with feet pointed at the rim (nobody will bite if your feet aren't squared), and at a realistic shooting speed. In all situations, never extend your

Shooting TIP

"For an efficient shot fake, just raise the ball to your nose/forehead area. Don't bring the ball too far above your head."

—Chuck Person

knees and raise your body; you must remain "loaded" to be able to react with an explosive move past the defender (see Figure 4.11).

Figure 4.11 Shot fake.

Three Fake Situations

1. Triple Threat Situation: Defender in Correct Position

This is a static situation because the defender is set right in front of you. Don't move the ball too much while making the shot fake; bringing it too high will not allow you to react and to put the ball on the floor quickly enough to beat your opponent. It should be a short pump to the forehead/eyebrow level at the highest. Then bring the ball down quickly to your hip/knee area for a quick first step past the defender.

2. Advantage Situation: Recovering Defender

You have either created a good lead or your defender is recovering, running at you to close out or block your shot. Raise the ball to a slightly higher point, over your eyes, making him think you are really going to shoot; your defender will probably compromise his position even more, raising his arm to block the shot (defender will be out of control). At this point, you just put the ball on the floor and drive past your defender.

3. Off The Dribble: Pulling Up

When driving to the basket (imagine driving, for example, from the wing at a 45-degree angle to the hoop) and you quickly stop to pull up, get the defender up in the air or off balance with a *short* pump fake. This fake will allow you to reestablish your balance and gather yourself to shoot comfortably.

Pump Fake

Kobe Bryant is excellent at getting his man up in the air with a solid pump fake. Then he can hit the jump shot, step through for a closer shot, or draw a foul.

SHOOTING WITH THE USE OF A SCREEN

Shooting off a screen involves more than simply catching and shooting after cutting off of a teammate's shoulder. It is a common but complex part of team basketball play that involves:

- Setting up your defender
- Moving without the ball
- Cooperation and timing with the screener and the passer
- Giving a good target
- Footwork
- Quick release
- Peripheral vision
- Reading the defense and reacting

Depending on how your defender decides to play you, and how well you, the screener, and the passer work together, you will have to find the best possible offensive solution. Even if you do not get your own shot off, maybe you will have drawn a defender away from a teammate who can now receive the ball in a better position.

Shooting TIP

"It's important to draw the defender's attention away initially. Take him one way, then change direction using a V cut in the direction of the screen."

—Glen Rice

Solutions, Depending on Defender's Position

1. Defender gets pinned on the screen – Pop out, catch and shoot. Use an inside pivot (see Figure 4.12).
2. Defender trails you – Curl tight and show inside hand as target. Use an inside pivot.

- Curl tight inside paint for a quick pull-up, runner shot, or layup depending how or if a help defender steps up (see Figure 4.13).
- Curl tight toward the elbow area for the jump shot (see Figure 4.14).

3. Defender goes over the top – Plant foot next to

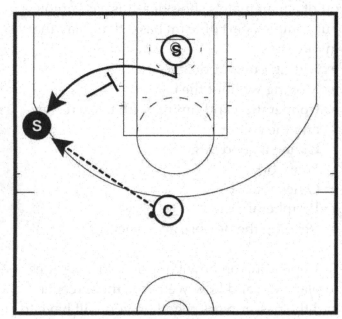

Figure 4.12 Defender gets pinned on the screen – Pop out, catch and shoot. Use an inside pivot.

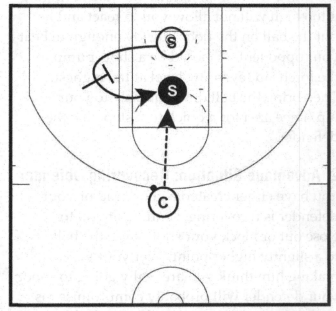

Figure 4.13 Defender trails you – Curl tight inside paint for a quick pull-up, runner shot, or layup.

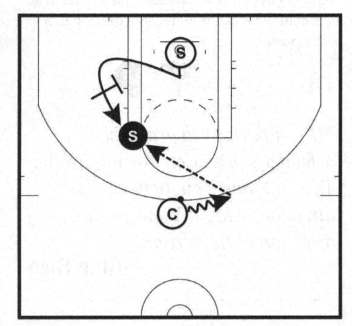

Figure 4.14 Defender trails you – Curl tight toward the elbow area for the jump shot.

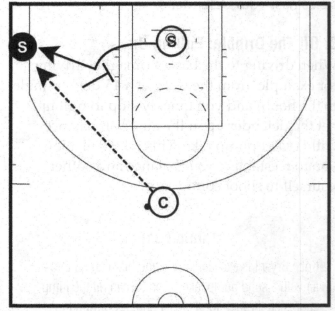

Figure 4.15 Defender goes over the top – Plant foot next to screener's foot, push off, and fade to the corner.

screener's foot, push off, and fade to the corner (see Figure 4.15). Use whatever footwork allows you to catch and shoot with the best body balance. I recommend using sideways, sliding steps instead of running backward or forward toward the corner. Avoid turning your shoulders away from the passer. Catch the pass as you drop into a jump stop on your reception. Your body's natural tendency will be to fade backward (negative motion), so you must try to compensate for this negative force, leaning slightly forward with your head, chest, and shoulders.

In this situation, the pass is rarely perfect; most times it will be a skip pass or an overhead pass that might be a little off-target. On your reception, try to face the basket the quickest way possible and with proper balance.

Key Points in Shooting Off a Screen

- Initiate contact with the defender.
- Raise the defender to the level of the screener or lead defender the opposite way.
- Use an effective change of pace—slow to fast.
- Time your cut with your teammate's screen. You don't want to be too early because you

risk a moving screen violation or the defense might anticipate the play.

- Come off your teammate's screen low and tight off his hip (lower than shoulder-to-shoulder) so the defender can't get through.
- Determine how the defender is playing you—trailing you, going over the screen, or running into the screen?
- Time your cut with your teammate's pass. Watch when the passer picks up the dribble.
- Show your hands, give a good target for the pass, and be ready to shoot. A good passer will try to feed you in front of your body unless the defender got through and is disrupting the passing lane.
- Good footwork allows proper balance and a quicker shot.
- Use your peripheral vision throughout your movement. You must see the defender(s), the passer, and other teammates. You should be able to realize right before you catch if you have enough space to shoot or if the screener has established good position inside the paint.
- Read the defense: be ready to make a quick pass or put the ball on the floor in case you can't get your shot off.

Shooting TIP

"It's very important to flex your legs and lower your body as you move toward the screen. While coming off the screen, I always try to square my body to the basket quickly while keeping my balance."

—Rudy Fernandez

Rudy Fernandez combines his agility with good technique and a quick release to be an efficient shooter off screens.

(Photo by Jesse D. Garrabrant/NBAE via Getty Images)

SHOOTING OFF THE DRIBBLE: THE PULL-UP JUMP SHOT

Being able to make spot-up shots in basketball is a huge asset because you can always help your team win games. To take your game to the next level, you have to become more of an offensive threat, developing the ability to get by your defender and pull up for a jump shot off the dribble. Your goal should be to become a shooter and a scorer.

The three-point line has really changed the game over the years, both on the perimeter and in the paint. Now, big guys don't play on the block with their backs to the basket anymore; they like to pop out for a three-point shot. Guards now shoot the three so easily it's like a free throw. Unfortunately, some abuse the three-point shot. When many players can't get their long-range shot off, they will try to attack the rim, driving all the way to the basket. Spacing principles have been compromised by this type of play.

Very few players today own an effective midrange game. Most perimeter players have the ability to shoot with range and get to the basket quite easily, but few know how to take a few dribbles and calmly sink a jump shot in the scoring area. An in-between game, with the ability to pull-up for a jump shot off the dribble from 10' to 15', is what separates the big-time players from the rest.

Shooting **TIP**

"A fundamentally sound player only needs two dribbles to create spacing to shoot."

—Chuck Person

The two greatest players of the last 20 years, Michael Jordan and Kobe Bryant, are examples of players who can score in many ways from dunking the ball to shooting the three-point shot. But Jordan and Bryant also are examples of excelling beyond the competition and achieving greatness with prolific midrange games.

Both a great scorer and shooter, Kobe Bryant's midrange game is virtually unstoppable. (Photo by Andrew D. Bernstein/NBAE via Getty Images)

How Can You Improve Your Pull-Up Jump Shot?

Shooting off the dribble incorporates most of the aspects addressed in this chapter: reception, footwork, and shot fakes, combined with good physical and athletic abilities that might allow you to beat your defender and shoot in traffic.

To improve your shooting off the dribble and develop a sound midrange game, key aspects and fundamental skills to work on and include in your everyday practice drills and workouts are:

- Ball handling: you must be able to control and protect the ball

Shooting **TIP**

"Whichever angle I'm moving at, getting my shoulders squared up to the rim is my main concern while pulling up off the dribble."
—**Chauncey Billups**

One of the best pull-up jump shooters in the NBA, Chauncey Billups has great balance and body control, plus an incredible ability to read his defender.
(Photo by Garrett W. Ellwood/NBAE via Getty Images)

- Footwork: 1-2 stop and jump stop
  - On your reception
  - Going up for the shot
  - Creating separation
- Triple threat moves/static one-on-one situations
- One-on-one moves off the dribble
- Cutting off your defender: "aiming" at the defender's shoulder/hip
- Ball pick-up from dribble
- Shot fakes
- Court vision/reading the defense
- Physical aspects: core strength, balance, agility, quick feet, and body control to be able to shoot with contact

Touch shots like "runners" and "teardrops" are valid alternatives to the classic pull-up jump shot around the paint. Some players have a natural feel for these types of shots off the dribble; they are hard to teach and learn.

When shooting on the move, both off the pass and off the dribble, your footwork options stay the same: you may use either an inside pivot (1-2) or a jump stop. The difference is that you are catching the ball off the dribble instead of off the pass. Therefore, learning how to pick the ball up from your dribble efficiently is of critical importance.

BALL PICK-UP OFF THE DRIBBLE

Ball pick-up is one of the most underrated aspects of shooting off the dribble. Good technique and practice will enable you to grip the ball comfortably and quickly so you develop a more efficient and faster shot release.

As you plant your inside foot and you square up to the basket, you must be quick, picking the ball up from your last dribble and bringing it into your shooting pocket. Pick the ball up between your knee and hip height.

Strong Side

Going to your strong side, your last dribble should be forceful so that the ball bounces straight into your shooting hand. Then you stabilize the ball with the balance hand to the side. Your body must be low with legs loaded, allowing you to pick the ball up at knee/hip

Figure 4.16 Strong side.

level. Square up your feet and body, bringing the ball into your shooting pocket, and go up for the shot (see Figure 4.16).

Weak Side

Going to your weak side is a different situation. It's a shorter and quicker pivot turn for your square-up because your lead shoulder is already pointing at the rim. That's why most players prefer shooting off the dribble going to their weak side. The pick-up this time is different since you must transfer the ball from your weak hand to your shooting hand. As you pick up your dribble from your weak side (knee/hip level), try to catch the ball on its side (as your balance hand should be positioned during the shot) and push it laterally to your strong hand, which is already cocked and ready to shoot (see Figure 4.17). This will quicken your release. Being "ball-quick" in this situation is very important. That's why your nondribbling hand is up for protection but should also be ready to quickly go up and shoot.

Don't reach over with your shooting hand to pick up the ball because you will then have to bring the ball back across your body, which could compromise your shot alignment. If you pick up the dribble *underneath* the ball and then bring it up to your shooting hand, you will end up having the balance hand in front of the ball and not on the side, thus interfering with your release. You do not want to make too many adjustments as you raise the ball because the adjustments will slow down your shot and probably not allow a clean release.

Figure 4.17 Weak side.

THE STEP-BACK JUMP SHOT

The step-back move has become one of the most-used and effective basketball moves to create space and get off a shot. Kiki Vandeweghe, the innovator of this technique (the "Kiki Move"), described it as a "defense mechanism" for himself, a slower-step player, against quicker, taller, or stronger defenders. Over the past 20 years, the more explosive players have taken this move to another athletic level because they can gain a significant amount of space on the step-back, really stretching the defense.

To execute this advanced move properly, you must have very good footwork and the ability to regain balance. In a halfcourt situation, this move is usually performed using one or two dribbles, as either your defender cuts your drive off or a help defender steps up. Therefore, even when you are practicing this move, you should work off both one and two dribbles. As your defender recovers, cutting off your path to the basket, plant your inside foot (closest to basket, most of your weight on it) and push off while stepping sideways at a 90-degree angle with the opposite foot. Next, bring your inside foot back with your body and both feet squared to the basket in a balanced stance so you are able to shoot (see Figure 4.18). Head, chest, and shoulders should be slightly forward to compensate for any negative motion or fading. Keep your feet low to the ground throughout the move.

Figure 4.18 The step-back jump shot.

Shooting **TIP**

"You must sell your drive and make your defender think you are attacking the basket in order to perform the step-back move."

—Kiki Vandeweghe

Kiki Vandeweghe creates space with his signature step-back move. (Photo by Dick Raphael/NBAE via Getty Images)

Although the steps are the same going to your strong and weak sides, there is a difference in footwork as you go up to shoot. In Chapter 1, you learned that to take a good, balanced shot, you should have a slightly staggered stance: your shooting foot slightly forward, your other foot's toe aligned with the instep. Let's compare the strong side and weak side step-back move executions:

- **Strong Side**—After you push off and side-step with your outside foot (your shooting foot), step back with your inside foot. The quality and length of this step will determine the quality of your balance and shot. There is more distance to cover here and more negative motion with the step-back because you want your nonshooting foot (inside in this case) slightly behind your lead foot. In addition, executing the move to your strong side, your shooting shoulder is farther away from the basket (not aligned) so your body has to "open up" in order to get your shoulders squared to the rim.

- **Weak Side**—This is the same execution as above, but your step-back foot (your shooting foot in this case) has to cover a shorter distance to end up slightly forward compared to your back foot. Plus, going to your weak side, your lead shoulder is already lined up with the basket, making both footwork and squaring up much quicker and easier.

So when performing the step-back move to your strong side, there is both more foot movement (approximately 12" difference in step-back length compared to moving to your weak side) and body movement—and risk of negative motion—making it a more difficult and slower move. Your body's balance is definitely challenged more. This is why it is much easier for a right-handed player to perform this move going to the left and for a lefty going right.

Many players today have developed even a hop-back move, which is essentially the same move, but it ends with a jump stop. These players have such strong and powerful legs that they are able to hop back and land in a jump stop and shoot. This is great if your body enables you to perform it, with the same advantages and disadvantages as the differences between the jump stop and the 1-2 stop.

OFF-BALANCE SHOTS

When a Kobe Bryant or a Dwayne Wade makes a turnaround fadeaway jump shot with two guys in his face, he makes it look like a regular shot. For fans, these plays are exciting to see, but it's not like the pros practice these moves. These are emergency shots that—due to these superstars' unbelievably superior physical and athletic talent—they are able to make…once in a while. But believe me, these phenomenal players have mastered the basic shooting fundamentals first, and they do not throw up a crazy shot unless they are forced to.

Unfortunately, many young players see too many "highlight" films and try to imitate their idols. Instead of noticing the pros' techniques and footwork, kids remain enchanted with the flashy stuff. The results are poor shot selection and improper shooting techniques. Even when they have an open shot or an open teammate, they try to take a crazy, off-balance shot that has no chance of going through the net (see Figure 4.19).

Don't hurt your shooting technique by trying to make flashy off-balance shots just to look cool! Your coach won't like them. So master the correct mechanics of shooting and become an elite athlete before you throw up a crazy shot while guarded by three players. And then, in an emergency situation as the shot clock expires, you might be able to score one.

Figure 4.19 Off-balance shot.

DEVELOPING A QUICKER RELEASE

Because of the level of aggressive defenses and overall athleticism, as an offensive player you must be able to get your shot off quickly and efficiently. Developing a reputation as a great shooter with a quick release will also open up more one-on-one opportunities for you and your teammates. Improving the speed of your shot execution depends mainly on what you do *before* you catch the ball, not on rushing your arm motion.

Key Points for a Quicker Release:
- Catch the ball "ready": in balance, feet pointed at the basket, legs loaded, and hands loaded with wrist cocked.
- Give a good target for where you want the ball; show hands (palms) in proper position.
- Jump behind the ball if the pass isn't perfectly on target.
- Don't reach for the ball unless the defense forces you to do so.
- Stay compact: eliminate excess motion.
- On the move: whether off the dribble or using a screen, always move staying low with your legs and hips flexed.

Shooting **TIP**

"A quick release depends on how fast you get into your foundation with your shooting hand correctly positioned on the ball."

—**Craig Hodges**

- Position the ball in the shooting pocket as soon as you catch the pass.
- Maintain smooth rhythm. No "choppy" motion.
- Don't shoot at the peak of your jump.
- Don't jump more than necessary and don't try to outjump your defender.
- Don't bend your knees more than necessary.
- Avoid a hitch or a prolonged pause at your release point.
- Avoid "dipping" the ball and "reloading" your legs on your reception.
- Use your peripheral vision to see how much space you have on your defender as you receive the ball.
- Without losing sight of your teammates' position on the floor, catch the ball with the intention to shoot.
- Use efficient ball pick-up shooting off the dribble.

INCREASING SHOOTING RANGE

In today's game, it is unthinkable for a perimeter player not to be a three-point threat, and for a big man not to be able to hit a shot from the elbow or short corner. Having good shooting range will force the defense to play you closer, which can open up your one-on-one game and also spread the floor for your teammates.

Shooting **TIP**

"On long-range shots, avoid releasing the ball at the top of your motion, but rather as your body is still extending."

—Craig Hodges

Shooting Range—What is your range? It is the distance from where you can consistently make a shot without altering your basic shooting mechanics. How do you know you are out of your shooting range? Even if you can make a shot from a given distance, you might realize that you are straining yourself or changing your form by compensating for a lack of physical strength or power.

Determine your range and the limits of it. One step at a time, move back and become comfortable with new distances, making sure that your shooting form remains the same. Once you've found the furthest distance from the goal where you still feel comfortable and do not need to alter your technique or strain yourself, you'll know the limits of your shooting range.

You can lift weights to build stronger legs, arms, and shoulders to be able to shoot the three-pointer more easily, but in reality, long-range shooting ability depends on more than one's physical strength because there are many strong players who have no range, especially big men. And there are also many seemingly weak players—Stephen Curry, for example—who can comfortably shoot from downtown without any strain.

How Do You Increase Your Shooting Range?

We will start by addressing the same principles we explained when talking about players with limited strength, as shooting range depends on both your power sources and your shooting form (mechanics and rhythm). Power, rhythm, and range are always closely related to each other.

As we discussed regarding rhythm, it's your legs that begin the shot motion, providing the initial push that must be coordinated with the swinging motion of the arms. Your shooting pocket and your point of release are two key ball positions in producing a fluid shot motion. Many times it is necessary to readjust these two ball positions, lowering them slightly in order

Shooting **TIP**

"Long-range shooting has nothing to do with jumping higher. However, leg and core strength are very important factors."
—Glen Rice

Glen Rice, one of the most dangerous shooters ever to play the game, shows his pure release on a long-distance shot.

(Vince Bucci/AFP/Getty Images)

to gain more rhythm and momentum for a longer-range shot.

You might have limited strength but an ability to use all of your strength efficiently to shoot even from long range because you have good rhythm. If you are strong but have a choppy rhythm, it will cause your mechanics to lose power during the shooting motion, limiting your shooting range.

While your leg and arm power seem to create the necessary force for your shot, it is your core strength that is the key to holding everything together. In fact, your legs would not be able to transfer the power efficiently to the arms if the midsection of your body (core) didn't stabilize the force transfer. Weak core muscles will cause a power loss during your shot motion, thus limiting your consistency and shooting range. In Chapter 5 we will discuss methods of improving one's core muscles.

Minor Adjustments That Will Not Affect Your Overall Shooting Mechanics:

- Flex your knees more (but never more than 45 degrees) to get the most out of your leg power.
- Use your feet. Extending your feet forcefully as they leave the floor is one of the most underrated factors in jump shooting.
- Don't shoot at the peak of your jump. Avoid unnecessary hang time.
- Don't jump more than necessary: from a longer range, you are probably going to have more time and you don't need to outjump the opponent.
- Lower your shooting pocket.
- Lower your release point.
- Make sure your shooting elbow is *in*: it will allow you to transfer power more efficiently into the release.
- Step into your shot motion: it provides more leg power, better rhythm, and momentum.
- Instead of a jump shot, shoot more of an elevation shot—a one-piece motion from

shot pocket through release point, shooting the ball as your feet leave the floor. This method produces a smoother, more fluid motion.

- Hold your follow-through. This is the last force applied to your shot. It makes a huge difference!

GAME SITUATION DRILLS

Footwork and Reception Drills

Zigzag with V Cut Drill

No ball is involved. This drill improves your change of direction, change of pace, and V cut technique. Use the length of the basketball court: take three to four steps in one direction, then shift sideways on your outside foot (your weight is now on that foot) and push off in a V motion, changing direction, thus creating a zigzag motion as you go down the floor (see Figure 4.20). Repeat in the opposite direction. Come out of each V cut using a change

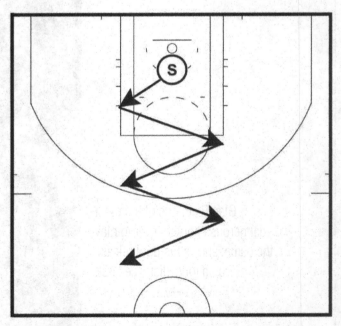

Figure 4.20 Zigzag with V cut drill.

of pace, and with your hands above your elbows showing your palms, ready for a pass. **Variation:** Zigzag with dribble, same footwork. **Note:** *This is a great drill to incorporate in your warm-up.*

Skater Drill

No ball is involved. This agility drill is similar to the previous drill, but you push off with a V cut on each step, moving side to side in a "skating" motion, shifting your weight each time (see Figure 4.21). This drill can help enhance your footwork in order to perform the "step-back" move. Remember to keep your hands above your elbows, showing your palms, ready for a pass. **Note:** *This is a great drill to incorporate into your warm-up.*

V Cut with Wing Reception Drill

Start inside the paint, near the basket. Imagine taking your defender one way, then jab with your foot closest to the basket and change direction with a V cut using a change of pace. Break out to the wing (within your shooting range) to catch a partner's pass from the top of the key area. Give a target with your hands in order to catch the pass in your shot pocket. Use a 1-2 inside pivot to square up to the basket (see Figure 4.22). This drill improves your change of direction, change of pace, V cut technique, reception footwork, and handwork.

Progression: Catch and square up only, in your triple threat stance, then add the shot. You can also work on your triple threat moves and pull-up jump shot off the dribble.

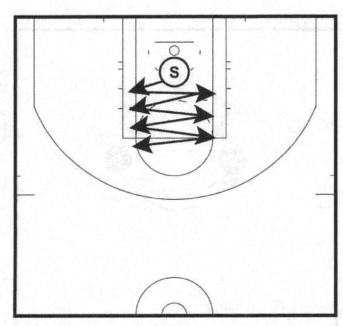

Figure 4.21 Skater drill.

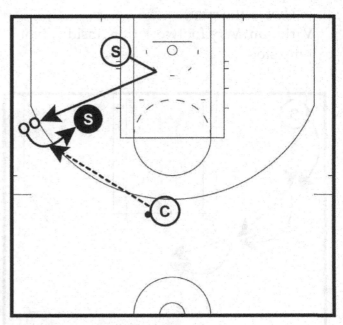

Figure 4.22 V cut with wing reception drill.

Around-the-Arc Drill

Begin at the intersection of the baseline and three-point line. Spin the ball to yourself around the three-point line (or around an imaginary arc within your shooting range) and catch the ball using proper 1-2 inside pivot footwork and handwork (see Figure 4.23). Perform in both directions. Work on your balance, catching with hands ready, pivot foot pointed toward rim, and getting "under" the ball in your triple threat stance.

Progression
1. Square up only, bringing the ball into your shooting pocket, triple threat stance.
2. Square up with shot motion – shoot to yourself.
3. Square up and shoot – shoot an actual shot to the rim.

Variation: Vary footwork from inside pivot to jump stop.

Figure 4.23 Around-the-arc drill.

Spot-to-Spot Drill

Move from spot to spot, back and forth using a 1-2 inside pivot to shoot off a partner's (passer/rebounder) pass. Set a goal of four to six made baskets. Your goal is to keep your footwork consistent, moving in both directions.

Variation: Perform with a jump stop; perform sliding from spot to spot.

Spots
- Corner to wing
- Elbow to elbow
- Wing to corner

Progression: Add dribble. See "Spot-to-Spot with Pull-Up Off Dribble Drill" later in this chapter.

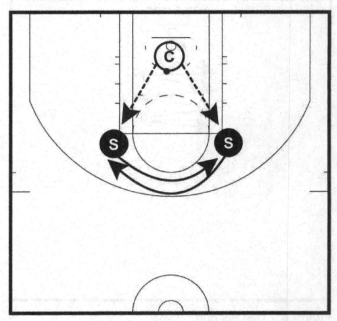

Figure 4.24 Spot-to-spot drill.

Self-Pass Drills

Spin the ball out, catch and shoot. Vary solutions for perimeter and post players.

Include movements off the catch and adding the use of a dribble, and practice all types of footwork (see Figure 4.25). Get creative!

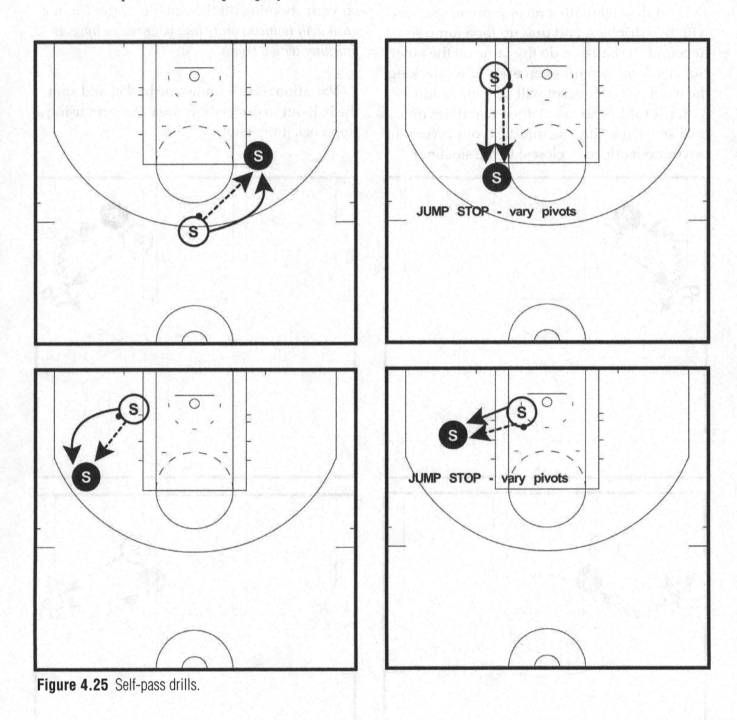

Figure 4.25 Self-pass drills.

Reverse Pivot and Crossover Drill

Spin the ball out to the wing outside the three-point line. Catch the ball with a jump stop and swing it through with a reverse pivot, crossover with two dribbles, and pull up for a jump shot. Rebound the ball and do the same on the other side. Perform two times on each side, attacking the baseline (your pivot will be your inside foot, closest to midcourt), then two times on each side, attacking the middle (your pivot will be your outside foot, closest to the sideline).

This drill is mentally challenging; it forces you to think about which footwork to use each time on each side because it is always reversed (see Figure 4.26). In addition, you will work on your shooting off the dribble. *Note: This is a great drill to incorporate into your warm-up, even finishing with a layup.*

Variation: Begin under the basket and spin the ball out to each elbow area. Perform using a step-back jump shot.

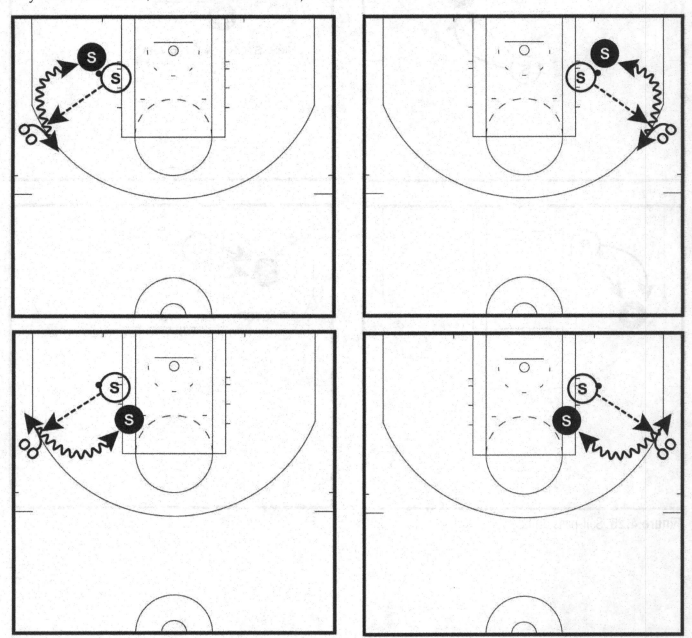

Figure 4.26 Reverse pivot and crossover drill.

Front Pivot with Pump Fake and Crossover Drill

This is a variation to the previous drill. Same setting, but now after your jump stop, face the basket with a front pivot and give a pump fake. Next, crossover with two dribbles and pull up for a jump shot (see Figure 4.27). Rebound the ball and do the same on the other side. Continue as described in the previous drill.

Variation: Begin under the basket and spin the ball out to each elbow area. Perform using a step-back jump shot.

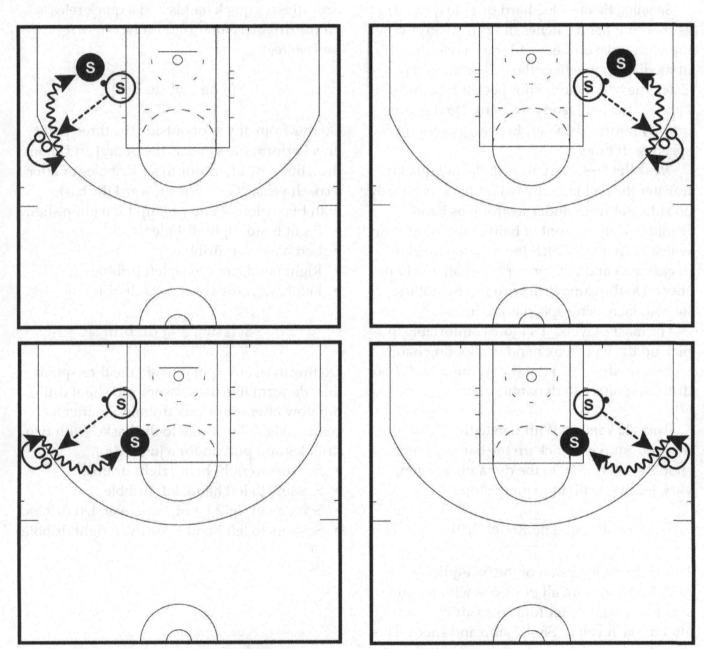

Figure 4.27 Front pivot with pump fake and crossover drill.

Drills to Improve Shooting Off the Dribble

Ball-Quick Drill

Stationary Version: In a basketball stance with legs flexed, feet squared, and body in balance.

Shooting Hand—One hard dribble (pound) as shooting hand catches the ball "ready" on top with wrist cocked, and the balance hand immediately stabilizes the ball on the side. Catch the ball in your shot pocket area and get "under" the ball, ready to shoot. Do the same drill with three dribbles. Repeat, increasing speed each time.

Weak Hand—One hard dribble and quickly transfer the ball laterally (so off-hand is already on side, not from underneath-up as hand would end up in front of ball) to shooting hand, which is "ready." Catch the ball in your shot pocket area and get "under" the ball, ready to shoot. Do the same drill with three dribbles. Repeat, increasing speed each time.

For most players, it's more comfortable to pick up the ball weak hand to shooting hand.

Progression: Add the shot (pound and shoot drill); stationary to dynamic.

Dynamic Version: With two to three dribbles forward, stop and pick up the ball. Add the shot. As a variation to the dynamic version, vary 1-2 inside pivot to jump stop.

Pound and Shoot Drill

This is the progression of the ball-quick drill. Perform from all positions within your shooting range. After four to six dribbles or after a coach yells, "Shot," stop and shoot. This drill stresses quick hands and a quick release off the dribble.

Scissors and Shoot Drill

This is a variation of the pound and shoot drill. Perform from all positions within your shooting range. Your legs move in a "scissor" manner back and forth while you pound the ball between them. After four to six dribbles or after a coach yells, "Shot," stop and shoot. This drill stresses quick hands and a quick release off the dribble. *Note: The drill becomes a leg workout too!*

Pound and Go Drill

Do this from any spot outside the three-point line. Perform the same as the pound and shoot drill, but now after four to six dribbles or after a coach yells, "Go," drive toward the basket with two dribbles and pull up for a jump shot.
- Right hand, right dribble
- Left hand, left dribble
- Right hand, crossover, left dribble
- Left hand, crossover, right dribble

Scissors and Go Drill

Do this from any spot outside the three-point line. Perform like the scissors and shoot drill, but now after four to six dribbles or after a coach yells, "Go," drive to the basket with two dribbles and pull up for a jump shot.
- Scissors to right hand, right dribble
- Scissors to left hand, left dribble
- Scissors to right hand, crossover, left dribble
- Scissors to left hand, crossover, right dribble

Around-the-Arc/Ball-Quick Drill

This is a cross between the around the arc drill and the ball quick drill. Instead of spinning the ball to yourself, take one to three dribbles and square up (see Figure 4.28). Focus on picking up the ball quickly from your dribble and squaring up for the shot. This drill incorporates proper footwork and handwork. Perform in both directions. This drill works on your ball pick-up technique while squaring up to the basket in your triple threat stance. Focus on pointing your pivot foot toward the rim as you pick up the ball and face the basket, while keeping proper balance with your body low and getting "under" the ball.

Progression
1. Square up only, bringing the ball into your shooting pocket. Triple threat stance.
2. Square up with shot motion – Shoot to yourself.
3. Square up and shoot – Shoot an actual shot to the rim.

Variation: Vary footwork from inside pivot to jump stop. Use one, two, or three dribbles.

Spot to Spot with Pull-Up Off Dribble Drill

Same as the original drill, but now add one or two dribbles and pull up for the jump shot. Reception is now outside the three-point line.

Going to the Outside—Catch the pass on the fly without stopping. Catch with a change of pace and pull up for a quick jump shot (see Figure 4.29). Vary one and two dribbles.

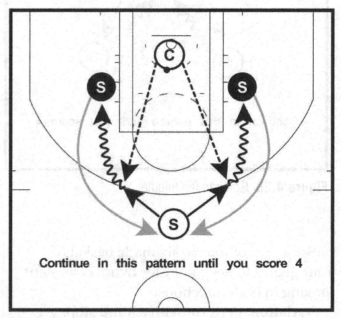

Figure 4.29 Going to the outside.

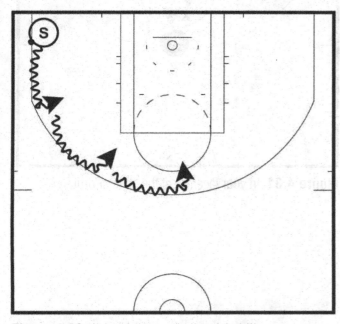

Figure 4.28 Around-the-arc/ball-quick drill.

Going to the Middle—Catch the pass using a 1-2 inside pivot, give a short pump fake, and crossover to the middle for a quick pull-up jumper (see Figure 4.30). Vary one and two dribbles. Move from spot to spot using a reverse V motion.

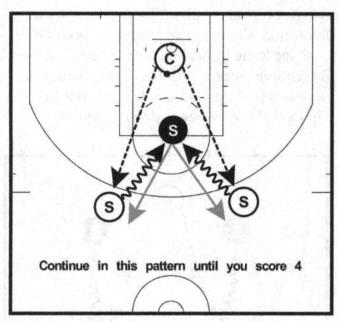

Continue in this pattern until you score 4

Figure 4.30 Going to the middle.

Set a goal of four to six made baskets. Your goal is to keep your footwork consistent moving in both directions.

Variation: Perform with a jump stop.

Progression: Perform using a step-back jump shot.

Spots:
- Corner to wing
- Elbow to elbow
- Wing to corner

Drills To Develop a Quicker Release

In Your Face/Run at the Shooter Drill

Coach/partner passes and runs *at* the shooter with hand high to disrupt. Shooter must get shot off quickly, trying not to get it blocked or beat the partner (tight off the hip to cut the defender off) with a dribble and pull up for a jump shot (see Figure 4.31). Change spots on the floor and adjust distances as you progress to make it more challenging for the shooter. Coach or partner can give different reads to the shooter: forcing weak side, one hand high, both hands high, running by the defender, etc.

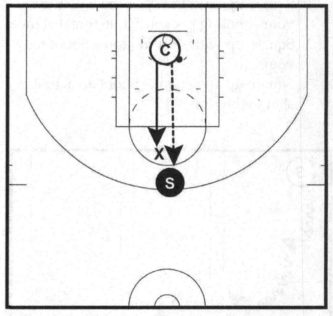

Figure 4.31 In your face/run at the shooter drill.

Quick Draw Drill

Shooter is in triple threat stance, ready to shoot with the ball in shot pocket, while coach/partner keeps arm extended with hand even with the ball, almost touching it. Shooter must rise straight up into the shot quickly as the defender raises arm and hand to block it (see Figure 4.32).

Progression: The defender can jump up to try to block the shot. Shooter can take one dribble to beat partner (tight off hip to cut defender off) and pull up for the shot. If the shooter is right-handed, the defender can make it even more challenging by using left arm and hand to attempt to block the shot.

Variation: Same setting, but now coach/partner challenges the shooter further with a close-distance bounce pass (short pass, almost "dropping" the ball in front of the player).

Figure 4.32 Quick draw drill.

Hand the Ball and Swat at It Drill

Coach/partner stands to the side of the shooter, then hands the ball to the shooter with one hand and tries swatting it away with the other hand (see Figure 4.33).

Variation: Same setting, but now coach/partner challenges the shooter further with a close-distance bounce pass, almost dropping the ball in front of the player. Coach/partner may change position also.

Two Ball Quick Shot Drill

Catch and shoot as another ball is being passed to you quickly (see Figure 4.34). You will develop a quicker release as you might not even see if the shots are going in. Concentration is also challenged as you must shoot and immediately focus on the next shot. Shooter must always be ready. One or two passers/rebounders.

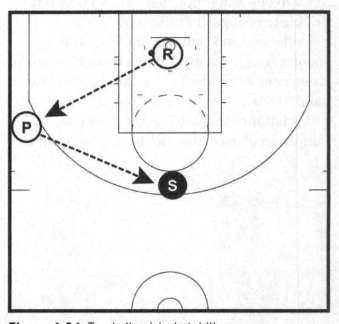

Figure 4.34 Two ball quick shot drill.

Figure 4.33 Hand the ball and swat at it drill.

Two Ball Quick Shot (Two Passers) Drill

This drill is best performed in a team or camp setting with two passers (one on each side of shooter) and two rebounders (see Figure 4.35). You catch and shoot from one passer, then receive another pass right away from the other side, over and over.

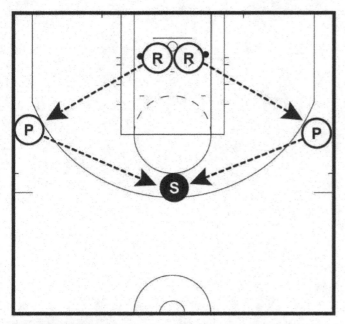

Figure 4.35 Two ball quick shot (two passers) drill.

Drills to Increase Shooting Range

These drills from Chapter 1, "Shooting Mechanics," also help to improve shooting range:
- Chair Shooting
- Floor Shooting
- Chair Shooting 2 (Rising Up)

Begin performing these drills inside your shooting range to get comfortable with them. Adjust distances as you progress and your range improves.

Progressive Set Shooting Drill

Part 1: Begin at the free throw line, shooting regular foul shots with your usual routine and technique. Your feet may not leave the floor. As you begin making baskets and feeling good about your shot, move back a step and do the same. After you start making shots from the new position, step back again and again, until you find the limit of your shooting range (the point when you begin altering your basic mechanics). This drill will force you to progressively use your feet and lower your release point and overall technique more as you move farther back. Make sure you keep your alignment and basic technique consistent. *Note: It is okay to fall slightly forward initially.*

Part 2: Once you reach the limit of your range using this technique, now add the jump into your shot motion. Still no steps, as your feet must remain planted as you receive the ball. Again, move back one step at a time as you become comfortable from each new distance, lowering your technique and getting the most out of your feet.

This drill will constantly challenge the limits of your range, and you will learn how to use your power sources efficiently.

Step-In Drill

This is the same drill from Chapter 1, "Shooting Mechanics." Receive the ball with your shooting foot back and step into your shot motion, getting maximum power and momentum from your legs. Have hands ready and knees flexed on your reception. Do not raise your hips, reload, or dip with the ball.

Chapter 5

The Physical Side

> *"I put as much work into my body as I do into my game."*
> **—Derek Fisher**

It's impossible to play the game of basketball at any level without being in your top physical shape. In order to become an accurate shooter with consistent form, be capable of getting open for a good shot, be able to perform under fatigue at the end of games, and avoid injuries, you must be an extremely well-conditioned athlete.

People assume that since shooting is less dynamic of a motion than a one-on-one move, rebounding, or playing defense, there is not a physical, athletic component to this fundamental. They are wrong.

This section focuses on these subjects and how they relate to the act of shooting:

- Strength and Core Training
- Balance
- Conditioning
- S.A.Q. – Speed, Agility, and Quickness

This chapter also introduces some basic body exercises and routines, with modified versions for beginners and progressions. It's a good idea to vary your exercise selection or routine to break the monotony and continuously challenge your body with new or different movements. As your body, overall strength, and conditioning improve, you will see how the gains will help your shooting form and shot consistency throughout your workouts, games, and season.

This is neither a conditioning nor a weight lifting program, but a series of body weight exercises you can perform on your own, either in your home or on the basketball court, *without* the use of any weights or equipment. Don't overdo your workouts in the initial stages of training. Focus on mastering proper technique first, then you may increase the number of exercises, frequency, and difficulty.

STRENGTH AND CORE TRAINING

The strength needed in order to improve your shooting technique and consistency is not the type you would associate with a body builder. The exercises include legs and arms but will focus on exercises that develop core strength, which will allow you to perform all basketball movements efficiently.

Core strength is closely connected to good body balance and proper movement. Ten years ago I had never even heard of the term *core*, now I hear it every day in the world of sports and fitness. What is the core? Defined as the lumbo-pelvic-hip complex and the thoracic and cervical spine, it is the place where all movement begins and where the body's center of gravity is located. The core is defined by the "stability" muscles—attached to the pelvis, hip, and spine—that are the foundation of our bodies.

Three Planes of Motion

In basketball, you must be able to move quickly and efficiently in all directions.

Whenever applicable, perform exercises in all planes of motion:

1. Sagittal Plane: front and back movement
2. Frontal Plane: lateral movement
3. Transverse Plane: rotation movement

Core Musculature

Core strength training targets the muscle groups of the trunk and torso that stabilize the pelvis, hips, and spine.

The major muscle groups of the **abdominal region** are:	The major muscle groups of the **spinal region** are:	The major muscle groups of the **hip region** are:
Rectus Abdominis – located along the front of the abdomen	Erector Spinae	Adductor Longus, Adductor Magnus, Adductor Brevis
External Obliques – located on the side and front of the abdomen	Quadratus Lumborum	Gracilis
Internal Obliques – located under the external obliques	Semispinalis	Pectineus
Transverse Abdominis – located under the obliques, it is the deepest of the abdominal muscles	Multifidus	Gluteus Maximus, Gluteus Medius, Gluteus Minimus
	Latissimus Dorsi	Tensor Fasciae Latae (TFL)
	Serratus Anterior	Psoas
	Rhomboids	Sartorius
	Trapezius	Piriformis
		Biceps Femoris
		Semimembranosus
		Semitendinosus
		Rectus Femoris

Figure 5.1. Core musculature.

Core Training to Enhance Your Performance and Jump Shot

This subject does not relate to shooting any more than other sport movements. But when talking about the foundation of shooting mechanics, it's important to know that a stable core can enhance your jump shot as you progress as a player. A strong and stable core will lead to:

- Improved balance, stability, and body control
- Improved stamina and endurance
- Greater efficiency of movement
- Greater speed
- Greater elevation
- Decreased risk of injury
- Correction of postural imbalances

In shooting, a strong core is essential for power transfer from the lower to upper body. A good shooting technique depends on efficient leg power and arm power to produce the necessary force for the shot motion. The legs would not be able to transfer the power efficiently to the arms if the midsection of your body (core) didn't stabilize the force transfer. If you have a weak core, only a small percentage of the force implemented by your legs will reach your arms, and your shot will be very inconsistent.

Shooting **TIP**

"A strong base and core will provide the balance necessary to shoot the ball properly."

—Derek Fisher

Derek Fisher, the ultimate professional player, shows a consistent shooting form thanks to his physical strength and stable midsection. (Photo by Noah Graham/NBAE via Getty Images)

Repetitive jump shooting can cause excessive or uneven strain on the spine. Strong core muscles can provide stability that can prevent pain and/or injury to the lower back.

Ray Allen and Steve Nash are good examples of players with strong cores, which can be seen in their movements on the floor and shooting motions. Both Allen and Nash have great body control, balance, an ability to absorb contact, and consistent form even when they are tired at the end of games.

A good basketball stance, in balance with legs and hips flexed, will activate your core muscles automatically. Having a stable base and midsection will relax your upper body, which is key for a smooth shot.

Core Strength Exercises

Core Stabilization

Prone

Face down on floor, elbows at 90 degrees under your shoulders, body resting on your forearms, fists, and toes (see Figure 5.2). Body straight, activate abs and glutes so your hips don't sag. Hold the position for 20 to 60 seconds.

Advanced version: Add movement with hip extension (10 reps each leg).

Figure 5.2 Prone.

Side

On your side, feet stacked, elbow under your shoulder, body resting on your forearm, fist, and feet. Other hand on hip (see Figure 5.3). Body straight, activating abs and glutes so your hips don't sag. Hold the position for 20 to 60 seconds. Perform on both sides.

Modified version: Hold the position two seconds, then lower your body to the ground, repeat.

Advanced version: Add movement, raising upper leg (10 reps each side).

Figure 5.3 Side.

Plank with Knee Tuck

In plank (top push-up) position, arms extended and hands under shoulders, body straight from head to toes. Hold the straight body position while driving your knee to your chest and back (see Figure 5.4). Perform 10 to 15 times with

Figure 5.4 Plank with knee tuck.

each leg. You may also perform this exercise in prone position, but inclined on a bench or step.

Floor Bridge

Lie on your back with knees flexed and feet flat on the floor, hip distance apart. Arms extended at your sides on floor (see Figure 5.5). Activate abs and glutes, raising hips so that they are aligned with shoulders and knees. Hold position two seconds and return to initial position.

Advanced version: One leg raised (10 to 15 reps each leg).

Figure 5.5 Floor bridge.

Table

Sit on the floor. Arms straight down, hands on the ground, aligned with shoulders, knees flexed and feet flat, hip distance apart. Raise hips so that your upper body is now parallel to the floor and perpendicular to arms (see Figure 5.6). Now your head, shoulders, hips, and knees are aligned. Your body should form

Figure 5.6 Table.

a table shape. Hold the position for 30 seconds without letting your hips sag.

Abdominals

Standard Sit-Up

On your back with your hands behind your head, knees flexed and feet flat on the floor, hip distance apart. Raise your upper body to your knees, with straight neck and back (see Figure 5.7). Return to initial position.

Figure 5.7 Standard sit-up.

Crunch with Feet Up To Sky

On your back, elbows touching floor and hands together on your sternum. Legs straight up, 90 degrees at hips, feet to the sky. Raise your head and shoulders, leaving your elbows in contact with the floor (see Figure 5.8). Return to initial position.

Figure 5.8 Crunch with feet up to sky.

In and Out

Sit down with hands on the floor at your sides, knees flexed, and feet together, lifted a few inches off the floor (see Figure 5.9). Extend legs straight out and then bring them back into your chest, never touching the floor.

Advanced version: Perform with hands off the ground.

Leg Thrusts

On your back with legs straight, arms at your sides. Lift your feet a few inches off the floor, bring your knees into your chest, and forcefully thrust your legs straight up to the sky, as your hips leave the floor (you can keep your hands under your lower back). Lower your body, in control, and extend your legs back out, without touching the floor (see Figure 5.10). Repeat.

Figure 5.9 In and out.

Figure 5.10 Leg thrusts.

Rotation Abs

Half Bicycle

On your back with your hands behind your head. Hips and knees at 90-degree angles. In a cycling motion, make contact with left elbow and right knee, then right elbow with left knee (see Figure 5.11).

Two versions: Quick touches or holding each touch two seconds.

Figure 5.11 Half bicycle.

Twist

Sit down with knees bent, feet raised a few inches off the floor, and hands together (you can hold a basketball if you like). Twist upper body, moving side to side, touching the floor with your hands each time (see Figure 5.12).

Figure 5.12 Twist.

Rotation Sit-Up

On your back with your hands behind your head, knees flexed, and feet flat on the floor, hip distance apart. Raise your upper body, twisting so that you make contact with left elbow and right knee. Lower your body and repeat on the other side, right elbow touching left knee (see Figure 5.13).

Figure 5.13 Rotation sit-up.

Lower Back

Cobra

Face down on the floor, body straight with arms extended out in front of you. Raise your shoulders and chest (chin tucked) as you open up your arms and hands with your thumbs pointed upward, contracting your lower back muscles (see Figure 5.14). Hold two seconds and return to the initial position. Lifting your legs off of the floor will give additional glute action.

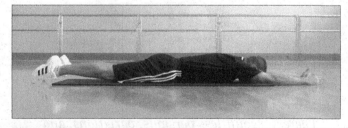

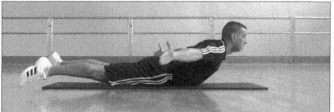

Figure 5.14 Cobra.

Superman

Face down on floor, body straight with arms extended out in front of you. Raise your shoulders, chest (chin tucked), and legs off the floor, contracting your lower back muscles (see Figure 5.15). Hold two seconds and return to the initial position.

Variations:

Half Superman—Legs stay in contact with the floor

Alternating Superman—Raise one arm with the opposite leg and hold two seconds; repeat, raising other arm and opposite leg.

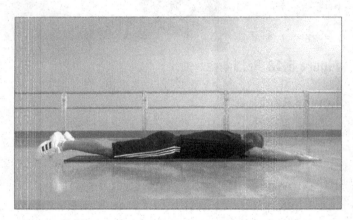

Figure 5.15 Superman.

There are countless versions, variations, and modifications to these exercises, so feel free to experiment.

Push-Ups to Develop Strength: Core, Arms, Shoulders, Wrists, and Hands

You do not need heavy weights, machines, or equipment to improve the strength needed to shoot the basketball efficiently. A classic push-up is the ultimate body and core stability exercise because it develops the essential strength needed to become a better shooter, both in your core and your arms, shoulders, wrists, and hands.

There are countless variations, modifications, and progressions to the classic push-up exercise. Vary your push-up routine. To avoid monotony and hitting a plateau, you must constantly challenge yourself to improve your total body and core strength.

Standard Push-Up Technique—Body straight, head to toes. Back, abs, and glutes tight. Hands under shoulders. Lower your body a few inches from the floor and push back up (see Figure 5.16). Maximum repetitions with consistent form.

Figure 5.16 Standard push-up technique.

Push-Up Variations

Wide Push-Up—Widen your hand position outside your shoulders.

Military Push-Up—Hands next to rib cage. Elbows close to sides.

Diamond Push-Up—Hands together, aligned with your sternum. Thumbs and index fingers touching, forming a diamond shape.

Decline Push-Up—Feet elevated on a step, bench, or chair. Progress first with two feet then one foot.

Finger Push-Up—Your weight on your fingers. Develops stronger fingers.

Stacked Foot Push-Up—Position one foot on top of the other. Change foot. This will challenge your body balance further.

Rotation Push-Up—After each push-up, with your arms extended, rotate your body 90 degrees and balance yourself with one arm raised in the air. Repeat on other side.

One Leg Push-Up—Keep one foot on the floor and the other raised in the air. Change leg.

Staggered Hands Push-Up—One hand near your rib cage, the other out in front of shoulder. Change hand position.

Clap Push-Up—Push-up explosively and clap your hands in mid-air each time.

Modified version: just push off the floor, eliminating the clap.

Basketball Push-Up—You may have seen this method with a medicine ball. Keep one hand on the floor, the other one on top of a basketball. Change hands. This version further challenges your shoulder stability.

If regular push-ups are too difficult, you can perform the modified versions:

1. Knee Push-Up—Standard push-up technique, but with knees on the floor.

2. Incline Push-Ups—Incline body, with hands elevated on a bench or a step.

3. Isometric Push-Up—Lower your body and hold the position, without pushing back up.

Get creative! Vary and mix up your routine, performing exercises at different speeds.

Leg Strength

Two-Leg Squat

Stand with feet shoulder-width apart and lower your butt under control as if you were sitting down in a chair until your thighs are parallel to the floor (knees at 90 degrees), then return to initial position (see Figure 5.17). Knees should be in line with your toes. Cross your arms with hands on opposite shoulders or bring your hands together for balance on each squat.

Plyometric version: After each squat, explode up, leaping off the floor.

Single-Leg Squat

Lift one leg and balance yourself on the other one. Hands on your hips (see Figure 5.18). Squat down under control, as if you were sitting down, and hold for two seconds. Come back up to initial position.

Progression: Touch the floor with the hand opposite your balance leg on each squat.

Figure 5.17 Two-leg squat.

Figure 5.18 Single-leg squat.

Wall Squat

Straight back against a wall, "sit down" so that your thighs are parallel to the floor, knees at 90 degrees situated above your ankles (see Figure 5.19). Hold position 20 to 30 seconds.

Variation: Squat on one leg while keeping the other one extended and parallel to the floor. Switch legs every 10 seconds.

Lunge

Step forward with one leg so that your thigh is parallel to the floor (knee at 90 degrees). Keep upper body erect, hands on hips, and back leg as straight as possible (see Figure 5.20). Push off your lunge foot back to initial position. Perform in all three planes of motion: sagittal (forward), frontal (sideways), and transverse (opening your hips and making a 45-degree rotation behind you).

Reverse Lunge

Same as a regular lunge, but step back with one leg instead of forward. This version puts less stress on the knee.

Figure 5.20 Lunge.

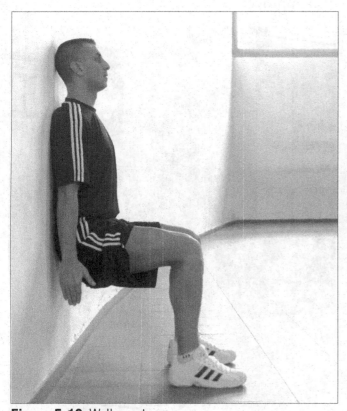

Figure 5.19 Wall squat.

Multiplanar Lunges

Hands on your hips. Each repetition consists of three movements:

1. Lunge forward (sagittal plane) and hold for two seconds. Return to initial position.
2. Lunge to the side (frontal plane) and hold for two seconds. Return to initial position.
3. Open your hips, pivot, and lunge out at a 45-degree angle behind you (transverse plane) and hold for two seconds. Return to initial position.

Perform sets of 10 repetitions on each leg. This is a great warm-up exercise.

Calf Raises

Stand straight with feet hip-width apart, hands on hips. Rise up, lifting your heels, balancing

Figure 5.21 Calf raises.

yourself on your toes. Perform 30 at a time: 20 at moderate speed, holding the position, plus 10 quick ones.

Variation: Single leg calf raise (see Figure 5.21). It's okay to help yourself with a hand on a wall for balance.

Other Ways to Increase the Strength Necessary for Shooting

Shooting Repetitions

You might not think about it, but the more shooting repetitions you perform, the stronger the body parts involved become. The more you shoot, the stronger you get.

Perform shooting repetitions within your range and gradually increase the distance as you become stronger. With time, your hands, fingers, forearms, triceps, shoulders, back, and legs will get stronger and your endurance will also improve.

NBA star forward Dirk Nowitzki is well known for his work ethic and dedication to shooting practice. (Photo by Jesse D. Garrabrant/NBAE/Getty Images)

Ball-Handling Drills

Ball-handling drills are important for mastering dribbling, passing, and catching fundamentals, but also useful for developing strength in your fingers, hands, wrists, arms, and shoulders (see Figure 5.22). In addition, you will improve your feel for the ball, which is crucial for your shooting development.

A good ball-handling warm-up is a great way to get your hands ready for shooting before a workout or actual game.

Ball-handling drills range from ball slaps and around-the-body circles to two-ball dribbling and one-on-one dribble moves.

Figure 5.22 Ball-handling drills.

BALANCE

The first shot component addressed in Chapter 1 was balance because it is the foundation of a proper basketball stance and shooting mechanics. Along with core strength, balance is the other key factor in performing all fundamental basketball skills quickly and under control.

Good balance allows you to stop efficiently at high speed and gather yourself or to square up to jump straight up for the shot. Body stability keeps you from drifting sideways or fading backward, hurting your accuracy. In addition, proper body balance helps you to land in control. Balance training will improve your joint stability and posture and decrease your chance of injury.

Body Balance Exercises

While performing balance drills, contract your abs and glutes to stabilize your hips, legs, and upper body, holding the position. Your balance leg's knee should be aligned with its toes.

Tree

Stand on one leg; place the sole of your other leg's foot on the inside of your thigh (see Figure 5.23). Hands can be on your hips or above your head. Hold the position 20 to 30 seconds. Repeat on your other leg.

Multi-Planar Balance Reaches

Lift one leg and balance yourself on the other. Hands on your hips. Each repetition consists of three movements (see Figure 5.24):

1. Extend the lifted leg forward, in front of your body (sagittal plane) and hold for two seconds. Return to initial position.
2. Extend the lifted leg to the side of your body (frontal plane) and hold for two seconds. Return to initial position.
3. Open your hips and extend the lifted leg behind your body (transverse plane) and hold for two seconds. Return to initial position.

Perform sets of 10 repetitions on each leg.

Figure 5.23 Tree.

Figure 5.24 Multiplanar balance reaches.

Single-Leg Squat

Same exercise as in Leg Strength (see Figure 5.18). Lift one leg and balance yourself on the other. Hands on your hips. Squat down under control, as if you were sitting down, and hold for two seconds. Come back up to your initial position.

Progression: Touch the floor with the hand opposite your balance leg on each squat.

Step Up to Balance

Stand in front of a step, box, or a bench (6"–18" high) with hands on hips. Step up with one foot, knee aligned with toe (see Figure 5.25). Push yourself upward, extending your knee and hip, while driving your opposite knee up (similar to a layup). Hold two seconds while balancing on one leg. Step back down with both feet to initial position. Perform in all three planes of motion: sagittal (forward), frontal (sideways), and transverse (start position sideways, then rotating into the step up).

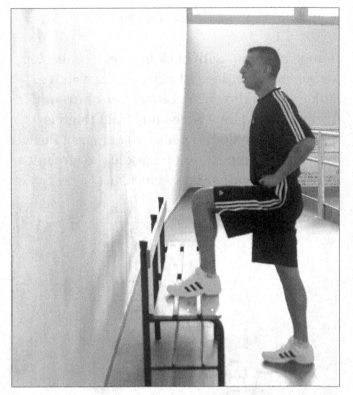

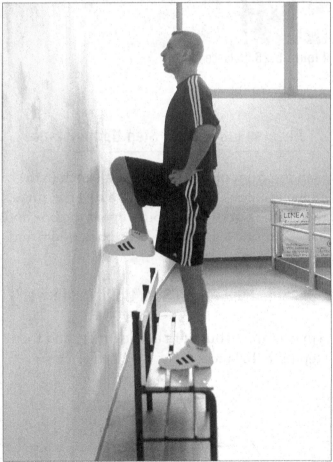

Figure 5.25 Step up to balance.

Balance Lunge

Lunge position, with back foot on a chair, step, or bench. Other leg out in front, knee above ankle (see Figure 5.26). Lower your hips under control to a point where your front thigh is parallel to the floor (knee at 90 degrees). Push back up and repeat. Keep back leg as straight as possible and upper body erect.

Figure 5.26 Balance lunge.

Reverse Lunge with Step Up to Balance

Stand in front of a step, box, or a bench (6 to 18 inches high). Step back into a reverse lunge, then come out of it, stepping up on the box and into your one leg balance. Step back down and repeat.

Side Lunge with Step Up to Balance

Same as above but with a side lunge, and then step up to balance.

CONDITIONING

A key part of being able to perform throughout the duration of a basketball game is your conditioning level. If you are a good shooter, chances are you will always be closely guarded and therefore you will need to move to get open. The best players at moving without the ball are rarely the quickest ones, but are the players who have great levels of stamina and endurance and know how to change pace and direction to set up their defenders.

Basketball is mostly an anaerobic sport because it is based on repeated short, high-intensity bouts of movement with brief recovery times. While it is only human to feel fatigued during an intense basketball game, practice, or workout, you must train your body and anaerobic energy system to recover quickly and to become the best-conditioned athlete possible. Basketball players hate running on the track or treadmill or even a few laps around the court to warm up…but give them a basketball and they may run up and down all day! The ball motivates players, as does the actual act of shooting. Incorporating conditioning into your shooting workouts will give you a good multipurpose training session.

Basketball workouts must be challenging and intense in order to reach high levels of conditioning. Include shots and moves off cuts, off the dribble, and off the catch that involve changes of pace and offensive and defensive transition. Get creative!

See Chapter 7: "Workout Drills" for information on how to incorporate the conditioning factor within your shooting drills.

S.A.Q. – SPEED, AGILITY, AND QUICKNESS

In sports, there is no substitute for being fast and being able to change speed, direction, and body position as quickly as possible in any given situation. In the game of basketball you are constantly using speed, agility, and quickness. Very few individuals are born with these abilities, so you must work on these aspects if you want to excel as an athlete.

As a basketball player, you must be able to run the floor and at a good speed. Believe me when I tell you that I've seen many professional players who *cannot run!* And at the same time I've scouted several very unskilled offensive players who have reached the NBA just because they can run up and down the court all day long. For a shooter, being able to run fast in transition or to an open spot on the court will give you a huge advantage and an opportunity to find good shots.

As a shooter, moving without the ball to free yourself to receive the ball is a key part of your game. You must be able to accelerate, decelerate, change direction, and stop quickly without losing your body control and balance. Good agility will help you beat your defender off the dribble, pull up for a jump shot, step back, hop, and readjust your feet and body at high speed or with contact.

Being able to react and change body position quickly in any situation is what separates the great athletes from the rest. This will allow you not only to free yourself to receive the ball or beat your defender with a quick first step, but also allow you to turn your body, get your feet ready, and elevate more quickly than your opponent.

You cannot play the game of basketball without being able to move your feet. As you improve your speed, agility, and quickness, you'll see how much quicker of a shooter you'll become.

S.A.Q. Drills

The following drills are excellent exercises for improving your overall footwork, speed, agility, and quickness.

High Knees

In your standard running motion, take short but quick steps, driving your knees up high (see Figure 5.27). Your arms (bent 90 degrees at elbows, close to sides) should swing back and forth in coordination with your legs' motion. Perform to halfcourt.

Figure 5.27 High knees.

Butt Kicks

Chest slightly forward, arms at your sides. Move forward, with a leg motion that alternates bending each knee backward so you are kicking your butt with your heels (see Figure 5.28). Perform to halfcourt.

Figure 5.28 Butt kicks.

Stairways

Use the stairs or bleachers at the gym or stairs at home. Run up the stairs, using short but quick steps and powerful arm action (see Figure 5.29).

- **Every Step**—Quick feet. Avoid stepping with your entire foot. Keep your weight on the balls of your feet.
- **Every Other Step**—More knee drive and longer strides.
- **Every Third Step**— Full running range of motion.

Figure 5.29 Stairways.

Quick Step Line Drill

Face a line on the basketball court. Start with both feet behind it.

1. **Forward and Back**—Step forward across the line in a 1-2 motion, with one foot and then the other; then step back to the initial position (see Figure 5.30, Diagram 1). Lead with the same foot going both forward and back. Alternate the lead foot each set.
2. **Side to Side**—Same as above, but in a lateral motion, stepping side to side across the line (see Figure 5.30, Diagram 2). The foot closest to the line will always be your lead foot.

Progression: Same drills but use a step or box instead of a floor line.

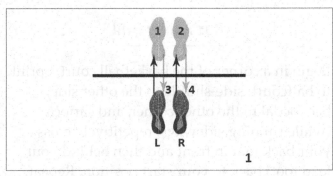

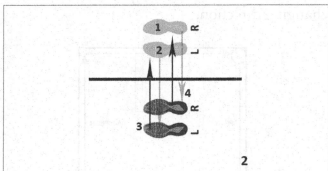

Figure 5.30 Quick step line drill.

Quick Hop Line Drill

Face a line on the basketball court; start with both feet together behind it. Perform these drills with quick feet and just a little knee flexion.

1. **Forward and Back**—Reactively hop forward and back across the line (see Figure 5.31, Diagram 1).
2. **Side to Side**—Same as above, but in a lateral motion, hopping side to side across the line (see Figure 5.31, Diagram 2).
3. **Rotation** (right and left)—Stand next to the line. Hop across the line, twisting your body 90 degrees, and reactively hop back to the initial position. Perform both to your right and to your left (see Figure 5.31, Diagram 3).

Progression: Same drills but with one-foot hops (single leg); two-foot hops up to a step/box instead of across a floor line.

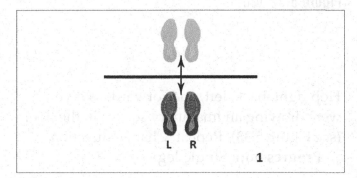

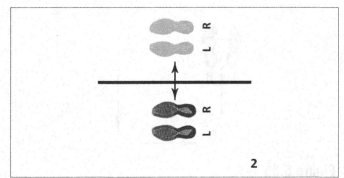

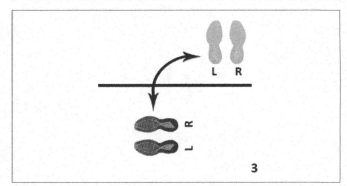

Figure 5.31 Quick hop line drill.

Cross

Hop forward and back, right and left, as if you were drawing a cross in the floor (see Figure 5.32). Repeat.

Progression: Single leg.

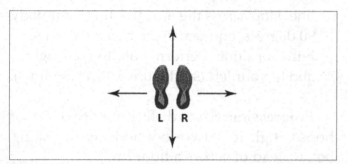

Figure 5.32 Cross.

Box

Hop right, back, left, and forward, as if you were drawing an imaginary square in the floor (see Figure 5.33). Repeat. Change direction.

Progression: Single leg.

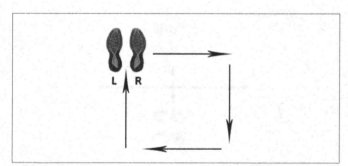

Figure 5.33 Box.

Nine Box

Begin in the middle square. Hop into each box, returning each time back to the middle one (see Figure 5.34). Change direction.

Progression: Single leg.

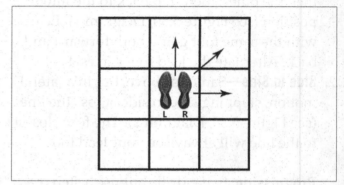

Figure 5.34 Nine box.

Box Agility Drill

Begin in a corner of the basketball court. Sprint to halfcourt, side-shuffle to the other side, backpedal to the other corner, and carioca (while running sideways, repetitively cross your back foot in front and then behind your lead foot) back to your start position. Repeat, changing direction.

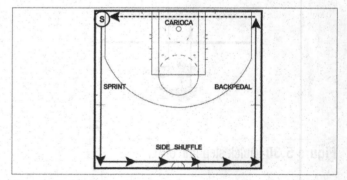

Figure 5.35 Box agility drill.

Get creative. You can make up your own circuit that mixes multiple S.A.Q. drills. In addition, you can incorporate S.A.Q. drills into your shooting workouts.

Fitness and Performance Tips

• Prepare your body before each workout, practice, and game with a good warm-up and dynamic stretching. Spend extra time using a foam roller (self-myofascial release technique) or performing some static stretching (see Figure 5.36) in order to address potential muscle imbalances or a particular muscle that might be tight.

Figure 5.36 Stretching.

• During your workout: while performing an intense one-hour-plus workout, team practice, or game, water is not enough to replace the body's energy and fluid losses. Sports drinks are recommended to give you the necessary carbohydrates and minerals to refuel during competition and training.

• Make sure you also dedicate time to stretching after your workout session. Relax your body with static stretching or use a foam roller to target those tender muscles that might need to be lengthened.

• Post workout: it is best to consume some sort of recovery meal, bar, or shake within 30 minutes of completing your workout in order to replenish your energy system and rebuild muscle tissue.

• Stay hydrated. Drink plenty of water throughout the day.

Chapter 6

Coaching
Shooters

WHO IS QUALIFIED TO TEACH SHOOTING?

The purpose of this chapter is to neither discredit nor diminish other coaches' theories and methods of teaching shooting. I do not presume to be the innovator of the only and/ or best system to improve players' shooting abilities. My intention is to simply share with other coaches the concepts and methods I have carefully developed, both on and off the court, that have brought successful results to the players with whom I have worked.

I have spent countless hours observing, teaching, and developing my concepts and I am continually seeking to learn more. My study of the art of shooting has encompassed the greater part of my life: first as a player, then as a professional scout, and now as a player development coach. Although I was a pretty good shooter when I played the game, I gained most of my knowledge about shooting after I stopped playing and began analyzing each aspect of this skill.

Thanks to the nature of my scouting job and my bicultural background, I have had the opportunity to observe some of the best coaches around the world and have been able to pick their brains and exchange thoughts, theories, and methods in regards to player development and shooting in particular. Over the past five years, working with players of all ages and levels, from NBA players to my eight-year-old daughter, I have consolidated all of the information I gathered and have developed my own concepts and teaching method.

A coach's attitude, personality, and demeanor are what draws a player's attention.

Assuming that you have some kind of basketball background and experience, playing or coaching, and that you know the basic shot mechanics, there are no mandatory prerequisites to begin teaching someone how to shoot a basketball. You have to start somewhere and then gain experience on the job while developing your own ideas and methods through observation and experimentation.

Your basketball background and your "shooting education" will determine your knowledge of the skill. Your knowledge, experience, and creativity will be your tools in developing a proper shooting program and selecting efficient drills. Your attitude, personality, and demeanor will draw a player's attention. All of these components, combined with work ethic and passion, will make you the best shooting coach you can be.

Personally, I consider myself an eternal student of the game and its fundamentals. I use a humble approach to teaching, as I know

Demonstrating proper mechanics to the player is extremely important.

I can learn something new each day in the world of basketball—watching games of any level, exchanging thoughts with coaches of any level or generation, and working on the floor with a player of any age. That's the beauty of the relationship with players: everyone is practicing, learning, and getting better at what they're doing. It's a two-way street. As a matter of fact, in this profession as in many others, the teachers learn from the students just as much as the students learn from the teachers. Every chance you have to coach a player should be viewed as an honor, a commitment, a responsibility, and also a great opportunity for self-improvement. Once you have a solid knowledge of the skill, the only way you are going to improve teaching it is actually on the job.

Shooting "Credibility"

There is no doubt that if you show you can shoot the basketball you automatically draw players' interest. If you've played in the NBA or at high level, you have instant credibility in the players' eyes, whether you can coach or not. But if you cannot teach and give them something new every day, after a while this "former player" effect will wear off.

Demonstrating proper mechanics and how to execute proper footwork or a dribble

move is extremely important. But you don't need to showcase your own prowess, proving that you can knock down every shot, rubbing it into players' faces, perhaps even embarrassing a struggling player. That surely does *not* improve the players' shooting. Whether you are a great shooter or not, whether you played in the NBA or not, it only takes a player of any age about 10 minutes to decide if you are knowledgeable and organized. Let your teaching do the talking, not your shooting. It should be about the player, not you!

Coach's Attitude, Personality, and Demeanor

Even if you are the most prepared and knowledgeable coach in the world, it might be your attitude, personality, and demeanor that earn a player's attention and trust.

Shooting **TIP**

"My coach should know my game well and know what to work on. I expect him to put as much energy into the workout as I do."

—Chauncey Billups

Everyone has his or her own personality and it's only human to have up and down moods. But if you show up to work without energy and enthusiasm, then players will also have less. Set the intensity level: during shot repetitions, competitive drills, and workouts you'll need to be more vocal, motivating, and energetic. Your energy will push players to give their best efforts. Count the number of shots aloud and push your shooter through the end of a strenuous drill. But during form shooting and teaching a particular footwork or move, you want to be calm, detail oriented, and slower speaking. Don't talk all the time. Let your shooter concentrate. Listen, have the player give you feedback, and answer all questions and address concerns. Teach, reinforce, and motivate. The players must have patience waiting for results; you have to have patience with their mistakes, questions, and sometimes stubbornness.

Some players are lazy and some need to be motivated and pushed. Having the right personality can be crucial to inspire and motivate. Your energy can be contagious with a player, a group of players, or an entire team.

Bonding with a player depends on the chemistry between the two of you. Players must know that you believe in them. Just because you are a good teacher and they want to improve doesn't guarantee the two of you will work well together. Be yourself, be professional, and bring it every day!

Get In Shape!

Coaches should also be in great shape, whatever their age. Unless you have a physical issue, you have no excuse. Being fit will automatically give you more credibility and a great professional image. Players respect and appreciate coaches who participate and are active on the floor during workouts and practice. Seeing that you are "into it," sweating as much as they are, will definitely strengthen your relationship because the players will realize that you really care and that you are in this project together. Whether it's demonstrating proper technique, driving and dishing, setting a screen, playing defense, or snapping a good pass, an active coach can make workouts twice as productive for players.

Being In Shape

Being in shape means you love what you do. And it will give you a longer career. Legendary NBA coach Bill Bertka is in his eighties, and after 60 years of professional coaching, he still has the body, passion, and energy to run all the Lakers' predraft workouts and to teach individual skills and moves to the players.

Now in his eighties, longtime NBA coach Bill Bertka has been passing knowledge on to players for more than five decades. (Photo courtesy of Bill Bertka)

DEVELOPING YOUR TEACHING METHOD AND SHOOTING PROGRAM

Three Stages of Training

1. Mechanics Practice
Mastering proper technique and correcting any mechanical flaws

2. Repetition Practice
Repeating the correct movement enables muscle memory to become automatic

3. Competitive Practice
Re-creating gamelike pressure shooting drills and challenges

The Shooting Progression Training Model was presented in the introduction of this book, and there are several references to shooting practice progression aspects throughout the first four chapters. As a coach, you need to determine where and how you need to begin working with your players. In fact, adopting this practice progression model as a reference, you will be able to design a training strategy that will allow the players to master the skill of shooting one step at a time, and then push them to reach their highest capabilities.

Stage 1—Mechanics Practice

This is the phase where you will be doing most of your teaching. It's in this first training period where you can stop, analyze, and correct, because you are not working at an intense physical level. Practice time is devoted not only to the basic shot motion mechanics, but also to breaking down any game-situation technique (footwork options, reception scenarios, one-on-one moves, pulling up off the dribble, cutting off screens, etc.) that the player needs to improve. Intensity level might not be high, but concentration level is. You will stress details and demonstrate and explain each aspect thoroughly to give your shooter the best

A vocal, motivating, and energetic coach will push players to give their best effort.

Figure 6.1 Mechanics practice.

> "When I played for the Chicago Bulls, our practice sessions were so intense and competitive that the actual games seemed easy."
> —**Craig Hodges**

shot off properly, in order to help take his game to the next level, you will need to challenge him through drills that re-create gamelike pressure and intensity. You want "game shots from game spots at game speed." During Stage 2 and Stage 3, you can't try to correct too many details because players are in game mode, focused on making shots. They will not be receptive, and you will hurt their concentration. You might point something out like "more legs," but don't stop the session to correct little things

shooting education possible (see Figure 6.1). If adjusting your player's incorrect shooting form is the main issue of concern, this first phase of training will be the foundation to development and it could be counterproductive to skip this practice stage.

Stage 2—Repetition Practice

You've addressed any mechanical flaw and taught the player how to shoot the ball and/or execute a move properly. This second phase's purpose is to get the player to perform as many repetitions as possible: shots and techniques. The more repetitions the player gets in, the more automatic the movement will become. Start being more vocal and motivating.

Stage 3—Competitive Practice

Now that your player has become a good shot maker with efficient offensive techniques to get a

Methods to make your shooting drills and workouts more competitive:

- Specific goal pressure – 10 made shots from each spot, for example
- Time pressure – a specific number of made shots in one minute
- A certain number of made shots in a row
- Finishing a drill with two to three shots made in a row
- Never miss two free throws in a row.
- Never miss three shots in a row.
- Defensive pressure – coach or teammate gives a "read" or provides contact
- Competing with a partner – two- or three-person workouts can raise level of competition
- Multiple reaction concept drills: two to three shot/move drills
- Adding a conditioning component to a drill, i.e., cut or transition
- Adding a defensive movement to a drill, i.e., defensive slide

like you would during mechanics training. Now is the time to push the player with your energy and enthusiasm. Competitive training is designed for the advanced player because it is technically, mentally, emotionally, and physically challenging. Most younger players (15 and under) may not be ready for this high-intensity level of training, so use your judgment on how or if to progress to this stage (see Chapter 7, "Workout Drills").

ESTABLISH YOUR METHOD'S AREAS OF IMPORTANCE AND MAIN CHECKPOINTS

What's important to you? My method's first objective is eliminating left and right misses, thus making sure the player's shot line is correct. My primary concerns regard:

1. **Feet:** Facing the basket. Balance. Shooting foot pointed to the middle of the rim.
2. **Shooting pocket:** Hold the ball with wrist cocked on the strong side of body. Ninety-degree angles.
3. **Good grip:** Feel the ball comfortably. Shooting fork in the middle of the ball, already pointing in the direction of the rim. No palm.
4. **Balance hand:** On the side, must not interfere with shooting hand release.
5. **Good follow-through:** Last force and direction to the shot.

I teach players to shoot the ball straight first, then worry about making baskets.

Check the Beginning and Ending of a Player's Shooting Form
When it comes to shooting mechanics, the most important parts of the shot are the beginning (loading) and ending (follow-through).

Be concerned with how players establish their base, with balance and feet pointed to the

---

Finishing the shot
A good follow-through can fix one or more flaws in a player's shooting technique.

---

rim, and how they hold the ball in the shooting pocket. Then check how they follow through and extend their feet on the release. The in-between defects should worry you less than the extremities (start and end). Even if players have a slightly flying elbow, if they finish the shot well, bringing it back in as they follow through, the shot might still be accurate. There is still a flaw that could be corrected, but it may not condition the shot as much as you think.

Establish a Comfort Level: Start with What the Player Does Well
When you observe a player's shooting technique, you'll probably notice the flaws first. Remind yourself to begin working with the player, acknowledging what he does well so that he feels immediately comfortable with you and your teaching method. The wrong approach will turn a player off.

Do not address all of the mechanical defects and needed adjustments at once. One flaw may be the cause of another one. Judge which issue should be fixed first.

Players might have had several coaches and received different—sometimes too many—methods of shooting instruction. The result is probably a lot of confusion with regards to how to shoot. Don't confuse the player even more. Keep it simple, especially with young players—don't overload them with information, detail and instructions. Address one or two aspects at a time.

"Keep it simple. When you get too complex you forget the obvious."
—Hall of Fame coach **Al McGuire**

Note: *It's easy to say, "Only one detail at a time and follow certain progressions." But chances are that you might have a player only for a short period of time, for example one week. You might be forced to address various aspects and try to correct multiple flaws during this brief time. It is difficult to obtain measurable results in one week, but you have to do your best to point the player in the correct direction. Try not to overload your shooter with unnecessary details; focus on your major checkpoints and give the player something to take home.*

YOUR METHODOLOGY SHOULD FOLLOW CERTAIN GUIDELINES

1. Scout your shooter
2. Develop a personalized program that fits your shooter's needs
3. Talk to your shooter
4. Educate your shooter

Scout Your Shooter

Whether he plays on your team or you are just working with him on his shooting, observe him and study him. Watch the player play in games and practice, in drills, and on his own: set shooting, in motion, and off the dribble. Identify what he does well, where he struggles, and when he hesitates. Get to know all his preferences and general tendencies. See what you can "keep" in his technique and what has to go. Pay attention to each component of his shot mechanics—feet, hands, alignment, follow-through, rhythm, etc.—and physical and athletic abilities. In addition, observe body language as this can tell you if he is a confident shooter or…lazy.

Essentials to Mastering a New Skill

In order to master a new basketball skill, a player must:

See it (performed correctly)
The player must see you demonstrate the correct execution of the skill. Show it in slow motion, step by step, and at game speed, making sure you stress the most important details.

Feel it (comfortably)
A new technique will initially feel somewhat uncomfortable to the player. Learning each mechanical part and understanding the motion's components through proper practice will help the player develop a better feel and become more comfortable with the new skill.

Repeat it (automatic)
Once the player understands the mechanical part and the motion begins to feel right, then the player must make it *automatic* through proper repetition. Begin at a moderate speed, then progress to repeating the execution at game speed.

Keeping in mind the Shooting Progression Training Model, where do you start and what should you start working on?

Develop a Personalized Program That Fits Your Shooter's Needs

Shooting is the first skill that a first-timer attempts. Making a basket is the most exciting part of basketball and is what attracts a child to the game. All young players have their own interpretation and personalization of shooting and develop their own style.

It is rare that all players learn and adopt the same technique and develop to shoot exactly the same.

As a coach, you can have the best teaching method for the perfect shooting form, but this might not work for all players. You can't expect every player to adopt the exact shooting technique you teach, even if it is

Shooting **TIP**

> *"Coaches must understand the biomechanics of each player's body. What might be fluid for one player may not be for another."*
> —**Chuck Person**

correct. You must realize and remember that everyone's shooting form will be different as each player's body structure is different in terms of height, size, strength, arm and leg length, hand size, shoulder width, etc. In addition, everyone has different levels of coordination and "feel" for the game. As a teacher, you must understand your player's body parts and perhaps even limitations (big guys and players who have had injuries). Adapt a shooting technique to each player's needs, based on physical structure and athletic abilities. Although all of the players' shooting forms might evolve in different styles, you should instill a few crucial and consistent guidelines: shooting fork in the middle of ball, alignment, and follow-through, for example.

Different shooters' individual physical characteristics might force you to tailor the best technique possible for certain players. Here are the most common modifications made to suit the needs of particular individuals:

- **Limited Strength**—Especially with younger players, don't be afraid of lowering a player's shot pocket and setting the release point to the clavicle/shoulder area, below the eyes instead of above. Have them use a step-in technique to gain more leg power. Landing slightly forward is okay. Jump shooting is not recommended for young players until they gain the appropriate strength.
- **Big Hands**—Less spread between fingers to make the player's hands smaller so that he

doesn't cover so much of the ball. Make sure this new hand grip doesn't permit any palm contact on the ball.

- **Long Arms**—Set the player's release point higher, above the head instead of right above the eye. Make sure they don't bring it behind their head, and that they keep the proper alignment.
- **Long Legs**—Shaky legs will cause knees to cave inward. Reduce knee flexion to avoid instability in the legs that will not permit proper balance.
- **Wide Shoulders**—Players are probably not as flexible in their upper body. Have them widen their shooting elbow out a bit because they probably will not be able to keep their elbows under the ball. Perhaps even a slight rotation of the body will be necessary in order to find a better alignment with the basket.
- **Past Injuries**—A previous thumb, wrist, shoulder, or elbow injury might affect a player's grip on the ball and/or shooting form. Evaluate which modifications you can adapt to the player's technique.

What is "perfect form," anyway?

Pick five great shooters of your choice. Let's take Peja Stojakovic, Ray Allen, Larry Bird, Mark Price, and Reggie Miller, for example. Each one possesses different size, physical and athletic abilities, and backgrounds. Do any of them shoot with the same exact form as another? No. They are all fabulous shooters, but none of them share the same "perfect form." While they do have some traits in common, they all have their own personal styles that were developed based on their physical aspects.

This tells you that there is no single perfect shooting form, and that each individual player will "personalize" his own shot. As a coach you must also try to "personalize" a shooting program that fits each player's needs.

Talk To Your Shooter

When it comes to shooting, players are very sensitive because they don't want to believe that they have a faulty shooting form. Players are afraid of change, even if it's in their best interests. Make them feel comfortable talking about their shot.

Without boring players, ask them questions. Try to understand if they realize what they are doing wrong. Ask if they've ever been told they do this or that in a certain way.

Players must know you care and most of all that you believe in them. Explain what you see and how you want to work together: where you want to begin, progressions, what they need to do, and how the adjustments will help their overall games and make them better players.

Explain that the adjustments will start feeling more natural with time and proper practice. It will take time to see results, so players must have patience.

Develop a relationship of trust, respect, empathy, and exchange. Have players buy into your teaching method. Don't allow the workouts and teaching to get too friendly because the concentration level will fade.

Ask players what they feel and what they think about when they are about to shoot the ball. Listen because they might have questions regarding a certain footwork, for example. Share what you believe is best. But don't try to force players to do something that doesn't feel right unless they are using a dramatically incorrect technique.

> "Kids don't care how much you know until they know how much you care."
>
> **—Unknown**

There is no magic in improving a player's shot. Both the coach and the player are going to have to *work*. Work many hours on the floor teaching, learning, perfecting, and correcting. But also work on developing a relationship and forming a bond.

Educate Your Shooter

The shooter is your own little project. Have pride in this project. Educate the player to the best of your abilities about:

1. **The Skill of Shooting**—Mechanics, footwork, and techniques.
2. **How To Analyze and Make Corrections on Their Own**—The knowledge players acquire will allow them to understand why they miss a shot and how they must adjust the next attempt.
3. **How to Study Other Shooters and the Game Itself**—Watching games on TV or live, more as a student than as a fan.
4. **Basketball Terminology That You Use To Teach**—The player must be familiar with all your "shooting words."
5. **The History of the Game**—Stimulate players' interest toward the game and they will love it more.

The ultimate goal of teaching shooting is not only for players to become better shooters, but also for them to learn to identify the reason they miss each shot that doesn't go in. This knowledge and experience will allow players to realize what felt wrong in the execution and then correct their own shots. Players don't have to learn everything you know about the art of shooting and teaching, but they should acquire a good amount of valuable information that will help their development as shooters. Great shooters learn to coach themselves.

Teach your shooter how to watch basketball games: observing how a player gets shots, moves without the ball, cuts off screens, the players' footwork, calling for the ball, etc. Ask players who they think is a good NBA shooter and why. What does he do right? Tell them to pay attention to the shooter's feet, hands, and cuts without the ball. Make them study the game, not trying to imitate the stars, but perhaps picking up things from players who have similar styles, bodies, and positions.

Most players today are not students of the game. They like to play, but do not *love* the game. They aren't particularly interested in studying the game, analyzing how advanced players perform certain skills and moves. They are not familiar with basic basketball

Teaching is the Best Way to Learn Something

While this statement is true for coaches, it is also true for players.

At the high school and college levels, it's a great idea to have your players work your basketball camps or to send them to teach at other camps so they can have an opportunity to coach younger players.

With all the knowledge you are giving them, they now will have a chance to teach those fundamentals they're learning to perfect.

Any opportunity players have to be involved with basketball will give them additional experience in learning and mastering a part of the game.

terminology and history—expressions, court areas, drill names, famous players, etc. If you give them drills or moves to execute, like the "Mikan drill," a "Sikma move," or a "Kiki move" (George Mikan, Jack Sikma, and Kiki Vandeweghe), they might have no idea who these former NBA greats are. Educate them. This will stimulate their curiosity and motivate them to learn more about the game. Growing up in a basketball family and learning to love the game has its benefits. Kobe Bryant is not only a phenomenal talent, but he was raised in a basketball environment because his father, Joe, was a professional player. He knows basketball history, the players on both sides of the world, and has been studying the game since he was a kid. Luke Walton, who has one of the highest basketball IQs in the NBA, is the son of Bill, who is an NBA legend, and all of his brothers also grew up playing the game. Basketball history can make players love the game more. As you start loving the game more, you'll be eager for more input and information in order to learn more.

The ultimate goal of teaching shooting is not only for the player to become a better shooter, but also to learn to identify the reason missed shots don't go in.

Who knows, maybe you will inspire a player to become not only a great shooter, but a future basketball coach as well!?

Unorthodox Shooters and Touch Shooters

Some great shooters have unique or unusual forms that might not be textbook methods. They could have a mechanical flaw in their form (flying elbow, excess or negative motion,

An unusual shooting form didn't stop former MVP Bob McAdoo from leading the NBA in scoring at over 30 points per game from 1974 to 1976. He shot over 50 percent from the field during his stellar career, in addition to winning two NBA championships, two Euroleague championships, and two Italian championships. (Photo by Focus on Sport/Getty Images)

ball behind the head, two-hand shot, etc.), but are still reliable shot makers. It would be almost impossible to teach these unique mechanics. Sometimes perhaps a simple fix could make them even better shooters, but if they can make shots consistently, they must be doing *something* right. I wouldn't touch those players' shots if they're successful. If it works, don't touch it.

Touch Shooters—What is a "touch shooter"? It's how I describe a player who might have an unorthodox technique or shoots every shot a little differently, but simply has an incredible touch and feel for the basket and is capable of making improbable shots. Such a player might have the unique ability to adjust a shot in the air or with contact, raise arc or point of release if necessary to avoid a block, etc. I wouldn't correct these players' forms. Sometimes overanalyzing techniques and little imperfections can complicate a player's confidence and development, ruining your relationship and trust level.

Can You Teach "Touch"?—I don't think a coach can actually teach a correct touch technique, but a player may be able to develop or improve touch through good practice habits, re-creating gamelike situations that call for a touch shot. As with runner shots, some players just have it. Others try and try but never develop that shot…. It can't hurt to try.

Correcting and Rebuilding Shooting Mechanics as a Player Gets Older

It is easier to teach shooting to young kids than it is to adult players. Young players might have not developed muscle memory in their bad habits, and their mechanical errors might be more easily corrected.

With older players, even NBA players, it's more complex. In fact, of all the fundamentals in the game of basketball, shooting is the toughest skill to correct in adulthood. Unless there is a minor flaw to be adjusted, you might have to break down the player's mechanics completely in order to make the appropriate corrections and rebuild a new technique. Professional players might have used the same incorrect technique for years and still have played at high levels. They could be in denial, ignoring the fact that they need to make a correction, or are simply afraid of change even if it's in their best interests. In fact, coaches and players are intimidated by the entire "changing a shot" process. Correcting a shot and developing a new technique is a complex process that requires dedication, time, patience, and often time off from playing five-on-five.

The Off-Season Is the Best Time to Change a Player's Shot

When players are working to modify and/or rebuild a new shooting technique, to get the best results, it is recommended they stay away from five-on-five competition. Improvement takes time because the proper mechanics must be learned before repetition instills muscle memory.

In real games, players can't overcome their competitive nature and will return to their habitual, incorrect shooting form, perpetuating the whole process. Committing to changing something that you have performed in a certain way for years is not easy. The coach and the player must be patient. A new shooting technique might not feel comfortable initially, causing a player's baskets made to actually regress for a while. The key is *patience*. This is the hardest part as the player might lose

confidence and become doubtful of the entire procedure. But as he starts feeling the new mechanics and seeing improvements, he will get excited and look forward to returning to the gym every day for more practice. As results come, so too does a boost in confidence. This is a crucial part in shooting development.

NBA veteran Michael Ruffin goes back to the basics during his off-season training. (Photo courtesy of Adam Filippi)

Shooting Drills Rules

- Don't miss two shots in a row.
- Never miss two shots exactly the same. Learn to correct/adjust right away.
- Don't say "no" as you release the ball. Think positively.
- Don't lose your cool.
- Focus on one shot at a time. Don't think about the total number or goal you're trying to reach.
- If you don't get your feet positioned correctly for some reason, don't throw up a bad shot. Instead, pump fake and gather yourself, reestablish your balance, and shoot.
- Always end with two made shots in a row.

Coaching Tips

- Include ball-handling drills in warm-ups so players develop a good feel for the ball.
- Begin shooting sessions close to the basket and progressively move out.
- Give great shooters high-level goals and challenges.
- Don't try to change a player's form if he makes shots.
- Don't insist on trying to help a player who doesn't show interest or desire.
- Don't compare a player too much to other players in the group or teammates.
- Don't say words like *change* or *bad*, but instead use terms like *adjustment* or *improvement* and *better*.
- Don't practice shooting with eyes closed. It's not realistic.
- Try not to correct each shot. Better to correct a flaw after several shots with same error.
- Don't underestimate the importance of the physical side in shooting. Core training should be an important component in your player's shooting program.
- Don't be afraid of having players shoot away from the basket (to themselves,

against the wall, etc.) if they need to make a mechanical adjustment.
- Flexibility – Don't insist on a drill if it isn't working.
- Know to end a workout when you notice a player is beginning to fatigue during repetition drills at the end of practice and consequently changing form. Practice is no longer productive at this point, and you should end the drill or workout. If you want to continue the shooting workout, move the player in closer and work on free throws or form shooting.
- Examine all angles of your shooter's technique: front (check shot line), back (check hips), and sides (check angles and stance).
- Especially with a professional player, establish a comfort zone before you begin offering corrections and suggestions.

Misconceptions

- "Hold the ball above the head." Ideally, you should bring the ball up to right above your shooting side eye.
- "Begin your shot motion from your shoulder area." Unless you are at least 6'7", it is very hard to create power and rhythm from that position. Start your shot in your shooting pocket (stomach/chest area).
- "Keep the elbow perfectly under the ball." This is not a natural position, and it might feel uncomfortable. The elbow can be very slightly out, as long as it is not "flying out" and it doesn't compromise your overall shooting alignment. A good follow-through will bring it in on your release.
- "Give direction with the index finger." Index and middle fingers (your shooting fork) should give last touch and direction.
- "Aim at a certain part of the rim." A mental picture of a perfect shot, with the ball right

above the rim just about to swish through, is better and is a positive image.

- "Bend your knees more." Do not overbend your knees (never more than 45 degrees) to gain more power because it will slow down your motion.

The Use of Shooting Tools and Devices

- I am not a fan of the "bigger ball." It's not realistic. It is a different size than the ball you play with, so it has a different feel, grip, and control than an actual game ball.
- I do like the smaller rim. The Perfect Jumper, for example, is a great tool that is ideal for good shooters who need a little challenge. This is better than the big ball. It is more realistic. The ball is the same, so the feel, grip, and control are the same. The new rim forces you to become a perfectionist, therefore challenging your aim and concentration.
- I am not a fan of toss backs or rebounding and passing machines. They are not realistic and give you a new image. It's better to work with a coach or a teammate. If you are practicing alone, you'll just have to chase the ball quicker and make shots!
- I have used the shooting strap, a restraining device that prevents your balance hand from twisting and interfering with the shot. I find it to be a useful tool if players can't stop from turning their off-hand and thumb into the shot.
- The heavy basketball is a good tool but not for actually shooting unless a player is right in front of the rim to develop a stronger

wrist. It's excellent for warming up with ball-handling drills and maybe a layup drill (the Mikan Drill with one or two balls, for example). It develops strong hands and fingers, as well as a good grip and feel for the ball, which are all keys for better shooting.

Choice of Drills and Designing Workouts

You probably have hundreds of shooting and workout drills. Now you have to decide which ones are best for each individual player and when to use them. You may design and develop a program of your own, but it should follow some type of progression and have guidelines. Depending on the level of your shooter, you will focus more on fundamental drills for basic mechanics or on competitive drills, which should be a mix of shooting challenges and "multiple reaction" drills. "Multiple reaction" is a concept developed by the great Bill Bertka to create drills that incorporate multiple situations, moves, and solutions at game intensity and game speed.

Make your workouts demanding, re-creating gamelike intensity. Training sessions must challenge players technically, mentally, emotionally, and physically in order to push them to the next level.

Be Unpredictable

Given that the game is unpredictable, make your workouts unpredictable as well. Throw in a surprise drill now and then, and/or rework the order of drills.

Workout Drills

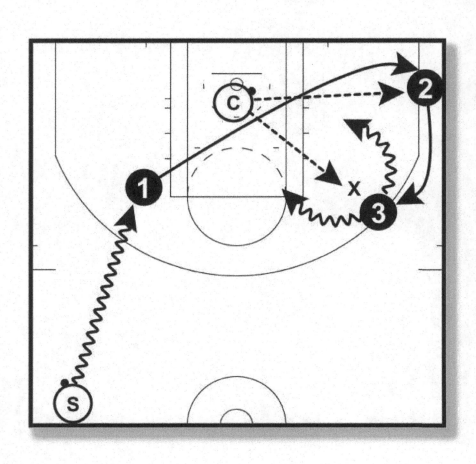

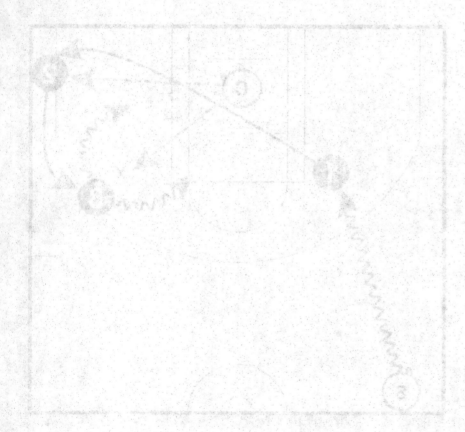

The best shooters don't just practice their shooting, they also *work* on their shooting. They always look for a new challenge and spend time on even small details that could give them a little edge. Whether it's a quicker release or a tighter curl off a screen, they know that at the highest level any small advantage can make a difference in obtaining successful results.

As mentioned in the introduction and in Chapter 6, during Competitive Training (the third phase of the Shooting Progression Training Model) workouts should be created for the advanced player who has already mastered a correct shooting technique and is ready to be challenged in more stressful drills that re-create gamelike pressure and fatigue.

Unlike the regular fundamental drills in Mechanics Training, where the coach and player take their time teaching, learning, and correcting, in these workout drills you must push hard. Coaches will correct major things, but will not interrupt the session often to do so because there is less teaching during this type of workout. These are intense, high-energy drills. Even if a coach tries to correct players

during this time, players will not assimilate the information well because their brains are in game mode.

If players begin to show signs of fatigue at the end of a workout, losing their legs and beginning to alter their shooting form, you should end the drill because practice is no longer productive. Move to a less intense drill, like form shooting or free throw shooting, or terminate the workout.

Training through high-intensity workouts is ideal during the summer period and/or preseason in order to get into the best shape possible for the upcoming basketball season. With some creativity, you can adapt these drills for your everyday practices.

Kobe Bryant's dedication and competitiveness make him one of the hardest working players in the NBA. (Photo by Noah Graham/ NBAE via Getty Images)

WORKOUT ESSENTIALS

Individual workouts and small group workouts (two to four players) must be designed with drills that challenge players:

1. **Technically**—to improve a certain offensive move, footwork, type of shot.
2. **Mentally**—to make players stay focused because they will have to react quickly from one part of a drill to the next.
3. **Emotionally**—to set and reach a specific goal, such as making a certain number of shots from different positions to end practice.
4. **Physically**—to add a conditioning factor in order to enhance stamina and endurance, which will help the players get in the best possible shape and fight fatigue. Improved conditioning will help players train better as they move forward.

Nobody Said It Would Be Easy!

The greatest compliment I ever received was unintentional. A veteran NBA player not known for his work ethic really struggled getting back into shape one summer. After about a week of working together, he was exhausted and said, "Adam, your workouts are not only so physically tough, but they are so mentally demanding!" Music to my ears!

I've always loved the concept of "Game Shots from Game Spots at Game Speed." Coaches must design drills that re-create gamelike situations and gamelike pressure.

Monotonous workouts will make the player lose interest after a while, so coaches must prepare several drills that develop the same skill. This way, players will always feel motivated and challenged by new and varied drills, and coaches will avoid boredom.

You must practice all game solutions:

1. Catch and shoot spotting up
2. Catch and shoot on the move
3. Shooting off the dribble
4. Transition
   - Catch and shoot
   - Pull up off the dribble

Perform all drills on right and left sides of the court.

Alternate strenuous drills with moderate-intensity ones. Players will run out of gas if you have them perform two or three demanding drills in a row. Always incorporate free throw sets (usually two at a time) between drills so players can catch their breath and practice foul shooting under fatigue. If you have two to four players in a workout, there is more rest time, but you don't want anybody standing around too long either. Make sure all players are equal level shooters, and if you must, lower the repetition numbers in order to have everyone move quicker.

Players must be mentally and physically tired after a training session is over. Workouts must be intense, more intense than actual games. If they don't train at high intensity levels (technically, mentally, emotionally, and physically), players' bodies and brains will never adapt to the game level's demand.

It is important that players feel even a small sense of accomplishment after each practice, finishing on a positive note and feeling good about their shot and their effort. Leaving the gym feeling confident will make players show up confident and excited to practice the next day. Never leave the gym on a missed shot or after not reaching the goal of a particular shooting drill (like 10–10 at the free throw line).

The workout drills in this chapter may require one player and a coach/partner, or two players and a coach. In any case, adjust them to any situation. Having a rebounder (another player or coach) allows the use of two balls, thus increasing the speed and number of repetitions for each player. The rebounder must feed the coach/passer as quickly as possible.

Get Creative, Coaches and Players!

Your workouts should include Competitive Shooting Drills (Challenging Shot Repetitions) and Multiple Reaction Drills.

Competitive Shooting Drills (Challenging Shot Repetitions) are directed toward reaching specific goals, such as a total number of shots made. Examples:

- **10 Made Shots** from each spot: Must finish each spot with two in a row.
- **"In a Row" Drill:** Goal depends on player's level. Begin with two in a row in order to move to the next spot, and progress to five. Midrange and long range.
- **"Swish" Drill:** Make five "only net" shots from all spots.
- **4+4+4 Drill:** Make four two-point shots, four three-point shots, four shots off dribble (two right and two left) from each spot.
- **1+1+1 Drill:** Make three in a row (close range, midrange, long range) in order to move to the next spot.
- **28/35 Drill:** From the seven perimeter spots on the court, you must make two in a row from each spot and return (14x2=28). You must make 28 before you miss eight shots total. You are allowed seven misses maximum. Your goal is 28/35, but you can change the goal number (higher or lower). This is a very challenging drill, ideal for ending your session.

Multiple Reaction Drills mix the skill of shooting with other fundamentals and conditioning, incorporating two or three different movements and shots in different situations. Examples:

- A dribble move with a pull-up jump shot; a spot-up shot; and a one-on-one solution as the coach will give you a read.
- A transition shot off the catch; a cut and shot off a screen; a spot-up three-point shot.

- A pick-and-roll pull-up jump shot; a spot-up three-point shot; a cut to the basket and finish with a power layup.

Shooting Repetition Spots

Perform your shot repetitions from the basic shooting spots on the diagrams, depending on whether you are a perimeter or an inside player (see Figures 7.1 and 7.2).

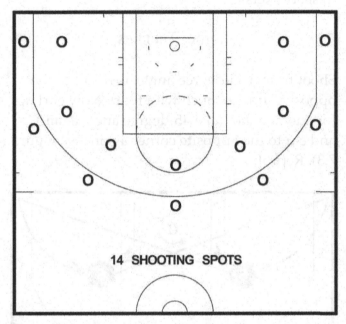

Figure 7.1 Perimeter player shooting spots.

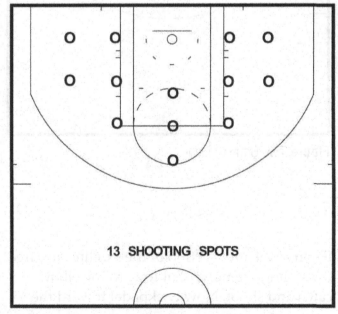

Figure 7.2 Inside player shooting spots.

WARM-UP SHOOTING DRILLS

These drills are to be performed in the beginning of your workout to warm up your body and get loose before stretching. Although they are designed as a warm-up and to be done at moderate speed, you can use them as regular workout drills by increasing the speed and intensity and setting goals (example: make four to six baskets).

Corner Touches

Shoot from a 45-degree angle, then cut to the opposite corner (touch with foot). Now curl up for another shot (at a 45-degree angle again) and cut to the opposite corner again (see Figure 7.3). Repeat.

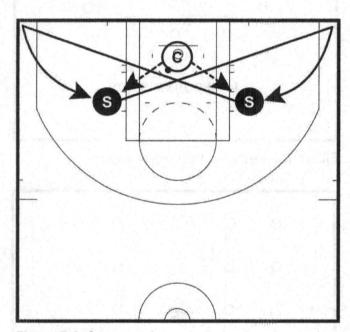

Figure 7.3 Corner touches.

Elbows 1

Begin at the intersection of the sideline and free throw line extended. Cut toward the elbow, catch and shoot. Now backpedal toward the midcourt line, return toward the elbow, catch and shoot, and run to the sideline (see Figure 7.4). Repeat. Perform on both sides.

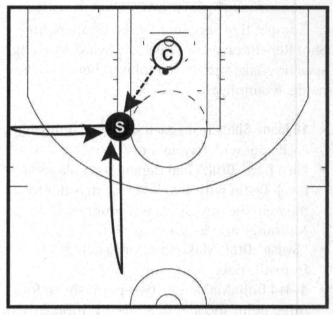

Figure 7.4 Elbows 1.

Elbows 2

Same as above but change side/elbow each time (see Figure 7.5).

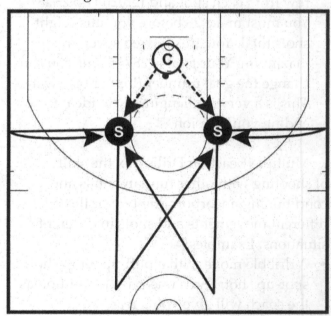

Figure 7.5 Elbows 2.

Give and Gos

Start in the corner and dribble up to midcourt. Turn and pass the ball to your partner/coach for a give and go (see Figure 7.6). Catch and shoot. Get your own rebound and repeat on the other side.

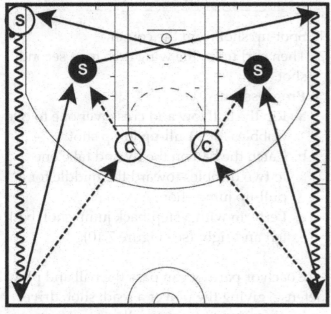

Figure 7.6 Give and gos.

Sideline Touches

Shoot from the middle of the paint, run to the sideline (touch with foot), and return to the middle for another shot. Now run to the opposite sideline and back for the next shot (see Figure 7.7). Continue in this pattern, progressively increasing the range of the shots up to the top of the key.

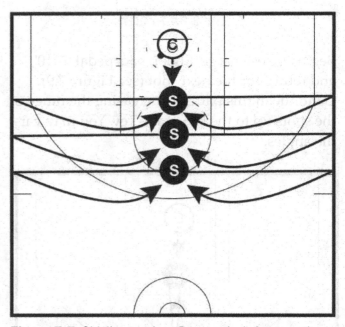

Figure 7.7 Sideline touches. Progressively increase the range of the shots.

Spot to Spot

Like the classic spot to spot drill (Chapter 4, "Drills"), but begin in close, moving from block to block. Progressively increase the range of the shots until you are moving from elbow to elbow (see Figure 7.8).

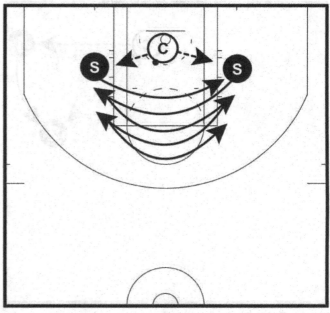

Figure 7.8 Spot to spot. Progressively increase the range of the shots.

Back and Forth

Begin at close range. Shoot, backpedal 8'–10', and return for the next shot (see Figure 7.9). Continue in this pattern, increasing the range of the shots up to the top of the key. You may vary the angles.

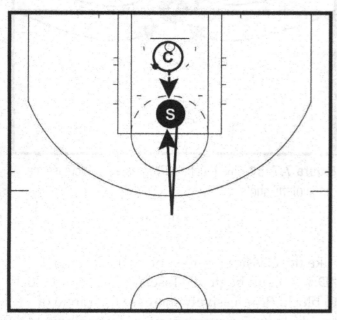

Figure 7.9 Back and forth. Progressively increase the range of the shots.

MULTIPLE-SHOT DRILLS

All drills are to be performed on the right and left sides of the court.

Two-Shot Drill – Corner and Wing

1. Spot-up shot from the corner.
2. Then curl up to the wing area for a second shot.
   Progression:
   a. Rip the ball low and crossover one to two dribbles for a pull-up jump shot.
   b. Catch the ball on the fly and take one to two dribbles toward the middle for a pull-up jump shot.
   c. Perform with a step-back jump shot, both left and right (see Figure 7.10).

Coach or partner can pass the ball and play defense, giving the player a read: shot, drive right, or drive left for the pull-up.

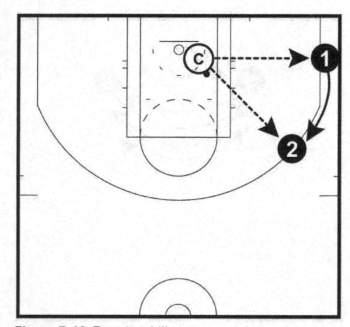

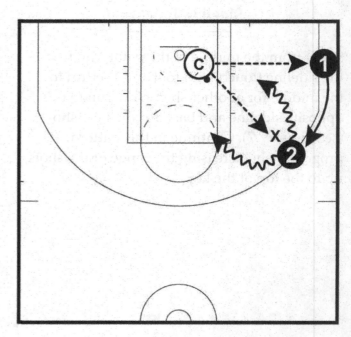

Figure 7.10 Two-shot drill.

Two-Shot Drill – Corner and Top of the Key

1. Spot-up shot from the corner.
2. Cut toward the basket and pop out, with a change of speed, to the top of the key for a second shot (see Figure 7.11).

Variation: Shots off the dribble.

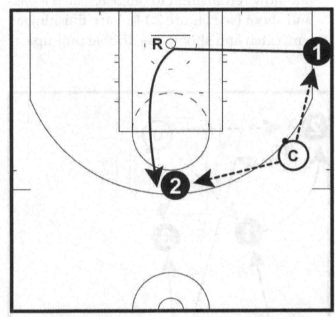

Figure 7.11 Two-shot drill – corner and top of the key. One rebounder and two basketballs required.

Three-Shot Drill No. 1

1. Transition shot (vary off the catch and off the dribble).
2. Cut across the paint and to the corner for a second shot.
3. Curl up to the wing area for a third shot: catch and shoot, one to two dribbles for a pull-up jump shot; or coach gives a read for a one-on-one solution (see Figure 7.12).

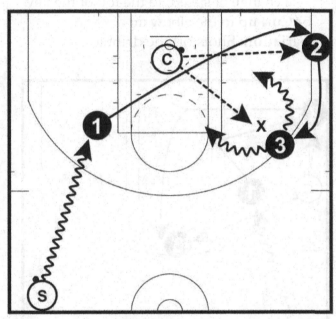

Figure 7.12 Three-shot drill No. 1.

Three-Shot Drill No. 2

1. Transition shot (vary off the catch and off the dribble).
2. Move toward the paint (imagine setting a screen or visualize "cheating" defender) and fade to the corner for a second shot (see Figure 7.13).
3. Cut for a third shot:
   a) Cut toward the basket and pop out, with a change of speed, to the top of the key.
   b) Curl up to the elbow area.
   Variation: Shots off the dribble

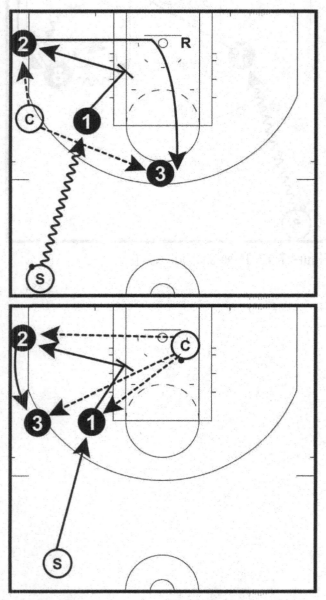

Figure 7.13 Three-shot drill No. 2. One rebounder and two basketballs required.

Three-Shot Drill with One-On-One

1. Transition shot (vary off the catch and off the dribble).
2. Move to the corner. Now coach/partner will pass the ball and run at you, giving a read: shot, drive right, or drive left for the pull-up.
3. Defensive transition, run to halfcourt circle and now retransition to offense. Catch a pass and shoot (see Figure 7.14). Vary finishing at rim, catch and shoot, one dribble pull-up.

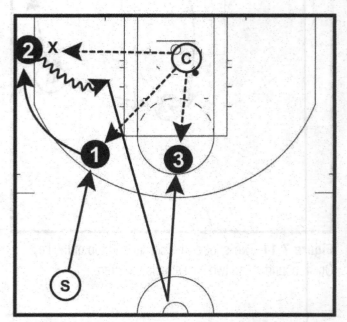

Figure 7.14 Three-shot drill with one-on-one.

Feed the Post with One-on-One

1. Feed the coach in the post and reposition in the corner: receive a pass, catch and shoot.

Variation: Change position of the "feed" to the corner and reposition on the wing.

2. Wait for a second pass, as coach/partner runs at you, giving a read: shot, drive right, or drive left for the pull-up (see Figure 7.15).
3. Defensive transition, run to halfcourt circle, and now retransition to offense: catch a pass and shoot. Vary finishing at rim, catch and shoot, and one dribble pull-up.

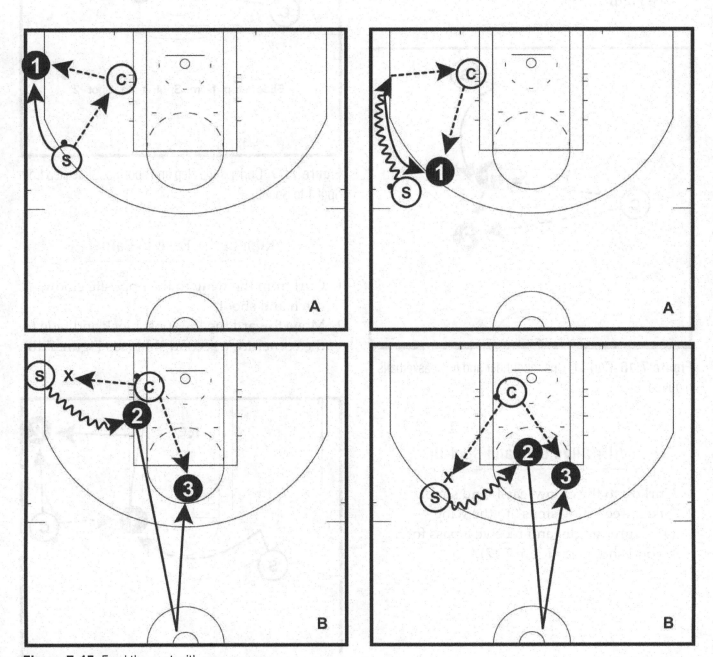

Figure 7.15 Feed the post with one-on-one.

CURL SERIES

Curl +1

1. Curl up to the elbow, catch and shoot.
2. Reposition for a spot-up three-point shot (see Figure 7.16).

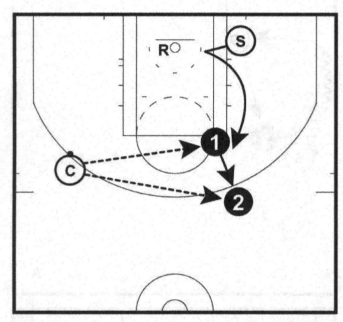

Figure 7.16 Curl +1. One rebounder and two basketballs required.

Curl + Slide Step and Spot-Up

1. Curl up to the elbow, catch and shoot.
2. Take three "slide steps" to the wing (45-degree angle) and receive a pass for a second shot (see Figure 7.17).

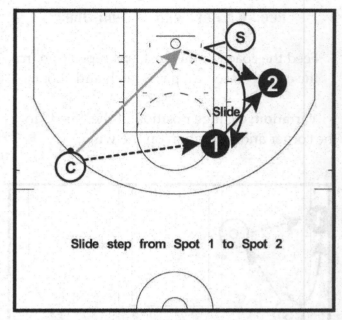

Slide step from Spot 1 to Spot 2

Figure 7.17 Curl + slide step and spot-up. Slide step from Spot 1 to Spot 2.

High Curl + Fade to Corner

1. Curl from the wing to the opposite elbow, catch and shoot.
2. Move toward the low-post block and fade to the corner for a second shot (see Figure 7.18).

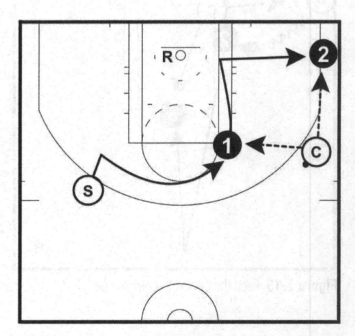

Figure 7.18 High curl + fade to corner. One rebounder and two basketballs required.

High Curl + Spot-Up

1. Curl from the wing to the opposite elbow, catch and shoot.
2. Reposition for a spot-up three-point shot (see Figure 7.19).

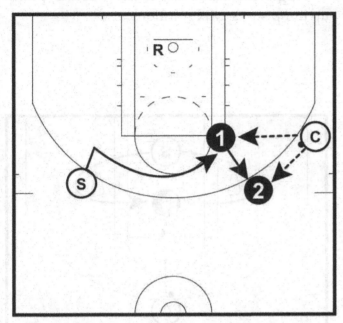

Figure 7.19 High curl + spot-up. One rebounder and two basketballs required.

Fade + High Curl

1. Come down the middle of the floor and pass to the coach/partner on the wing. Imagine your defender "cheating" so you don't cut in front for a return pass, now fade toward the opposite elbow to catch and shoot (see Figure 7.20).
2. Now, curl back toward the opposite elbow for another shot (on the catch or adding one dribble).

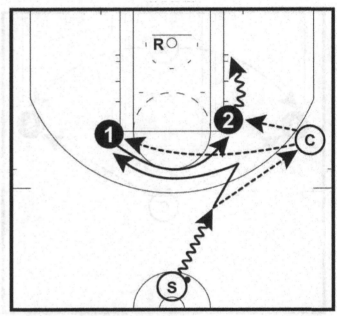

Figure 7.20 Fade + high curl. One rebounder and two basketballs required.

SHOOTING OFF SCREENS

4x4 Series

Start under the basket and cut off a screen (chair, teammate, or coach) to catch and shoot. Move back into the paint and do the same to the opposite side. Continue until you have scored four baskets. Practice all solutions (see Figure 7.21):

- Pop out (defender gets pinned)
- Curl to elbow
- Tight curl to middle of paint (vary with runner shot or add a step-back)
- Fade to corner

Progression: Add one to two dribbles, pull-up jump shots. Mix solutions.

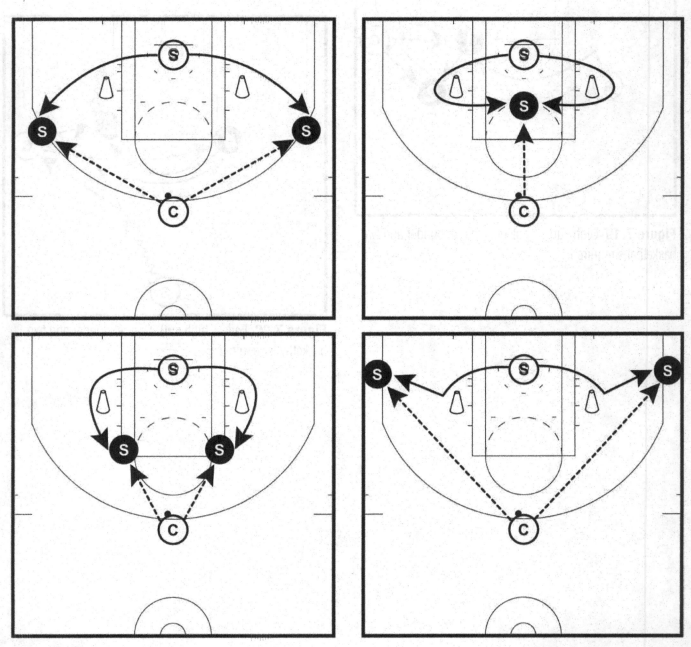

Figure 7.21 4x4 series.

Screen +1

1. Cut off the screen, catch and shoot.
2. Run toward the corner, then change speed and direction, catching and shooting a second shot in the top of the key area (see Figure 7.22).

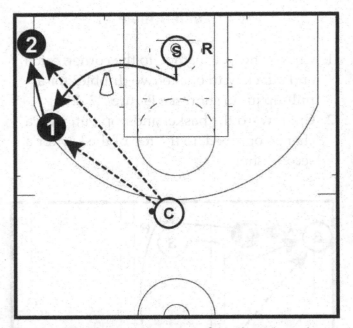

Figure 7.23 Screen +1 in corner. One rebounder and two basketballs required.

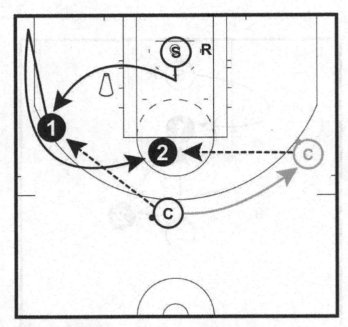

Figure 7.22 Screen +1. One rebounder and two basketballs required.

Screen +1 in Corner

1. Cut off the screen, catch and shoot.
2. Reposition in corner for a spot-up shot (see Figure 7.23).

Fade + Hand-Off

1. Cut off the screen, fade to the corner, catch and shoot.
2. Now coach/partner will dribble toward you for a hand-off pass: catch and drive off tight for a pull-up jump shot (see Figure 7.24).

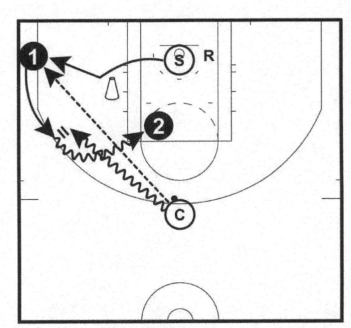

Figure 7.24 Fade + hand-off. One rebounder and two basketballs required.

Fade with Dribble +1

1. Cut off the screen, fade to the corner, catch and attack with one to two dribbles for a pull-up jump shot (see Figure 7.25).
2. Cut toward the basket and pop out, with a change of speed, to the top of the key for a second shot.

Tight Curl +1

1. Cut off the screen and curl tight into the paint for a short jump shot (or runner shot).
2. Reposition to the top of the key area for a spot-up three-point shot (see Figure 7.26).

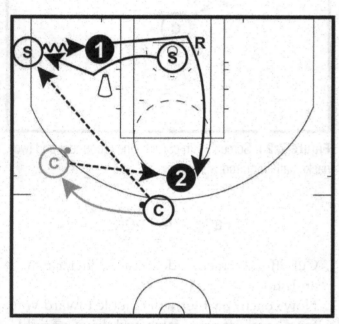

Figure 7.25 Fade with dribble +1. One rebounder and two basketballs required.

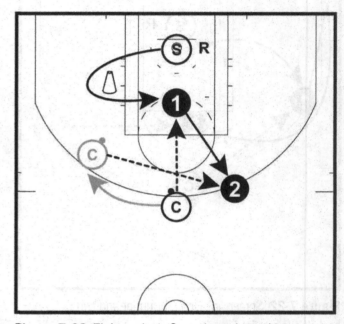

Figure 7.26 Tight curl +1. One rebounder and two basketballs required.

TRANSITION DRILLS

Transition Shot (Middle) + One-On-One

1. Run down the middle, catch and shoot off coach/partner's pass.
2. Run and touch the sideline, change speed and direction, receive a pass from coach/partner, who now becomes defender (see Figure 7.27). Attack one-on-one, reading defender's position.

Transition Shot (Wing) + One-on-One

1. Run on the wing, catch and shoot off coach/partner's pass.
2. Run toward the corner, change speed and direction, receive a pass from coach/partner who now becomes defender (see Figure 7.28). Attack one-on-one, reading defender's position.

Variation: Perform the transition shot off the dribble.

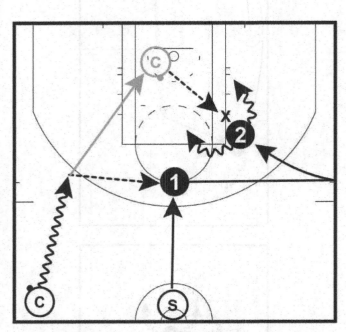

Figure 7.27 Transition shot (middle) + one-on-one.

Figure 7.28 Transition shot (wing) + one-on-one.

Dribble Move/Pull-Up + Mid-Post Shot

1. Perform a dribble move and pull up for the jump shot (see Figure 7.29).
2. Cut toward the basket and pop-out to the opposite side to receive a pass. Execute a turnaround jump shot or face-up and take one to two dribbles for the pull-up.

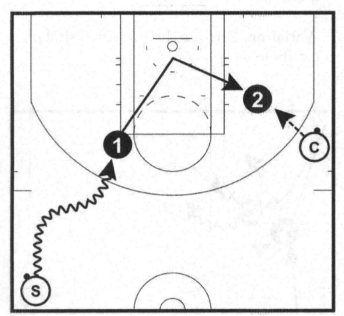

Figure 7.29 Dribble move/pull-up + mid-post shot. Shooter can get own rebound after first shot, or you can have a rebounder and two basketballs.

Transition 4x4 Series

With a coach/partner. Begin at midcourt: running in transition back and forth, catch and shoot until you score four baskets. Practice all solutions from both wing and middle (see Figure 7.30):

- Two-point shots
- Three-point shots
- "Rip" plus one to two dribbles right for pull-up jump shots (add step-back)
- "Rip" plus one to two dribbles left for pull-up jump shots (add step-back)

Note: *This drill can be performed with a coach/partner running the fast break and passing to the shooter or simply having a passer/rebounder at each basket. Coaches may prefer to have a player handling the ball and feeding the shooter in order to have players work on more aspects.*

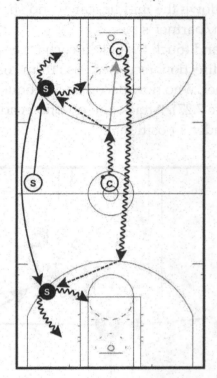

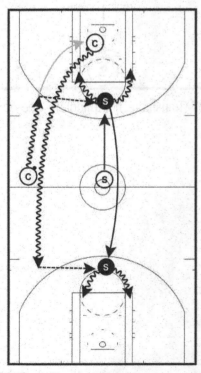

Figure 7.30 Transition 4x4 series.

PICK-AND-ROLL DRILLS

Note: I prefer to use a chair as the "screener" and a coach as the defender in order to give the player a read:

- If coach plays "soft" or goes "under" the screen, shoot in his face.
- If coach trails you off the screen, you should cut off the chair tight.
- If coach is in proper position, use a step-back move.
- If coach is really aggressive, use two to three retreat dribbles to create space, then attack him.
- If coach comes out as a help defender, you will split the trap.

Side Pick-and-Roll + Spot-Up

1. Side pick-and-roll for a pull-up jump shot (see Figure 7.31).
2. Reposition to the top of the key area for a spot-up shot.

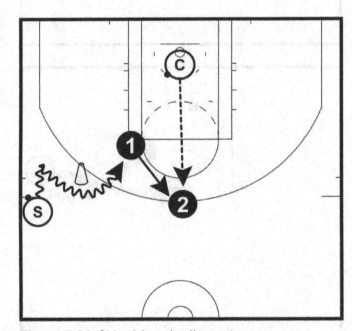

Figure 7.31 Side pick-and-roll + spot-up.

Middle Pick-and-Roll + Spot-Up

1. Middle pick-and-roll for a pull-up jump shot (see Figure 7.32).
2. Reposition to the wing area for a spot-up shot.

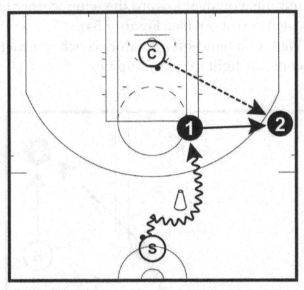

Figure 7.32 Middle pick-and-roll + spot-up.

Corner Pick-and-Roll + Transition

1. Pick-and-roll with coach from the corner, pull-up jump shot (see Figure 7.33).
2. Run to midcourt and retransition to offense for a second shot; catch and shoot or one-on-one solution against coach.

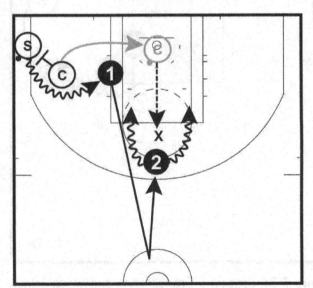

Figure 7.33 Corner pick-and-roll + transition.

SPACING DRILLS

Spacing 1

1. While coach/partner penetrates toward the middle, you drift toward the wing/corner to catch and shoot (see Figure 7.34).
2. Wait for a hand-off pass from coach/partner, come off tight for a pull-up jump shot.

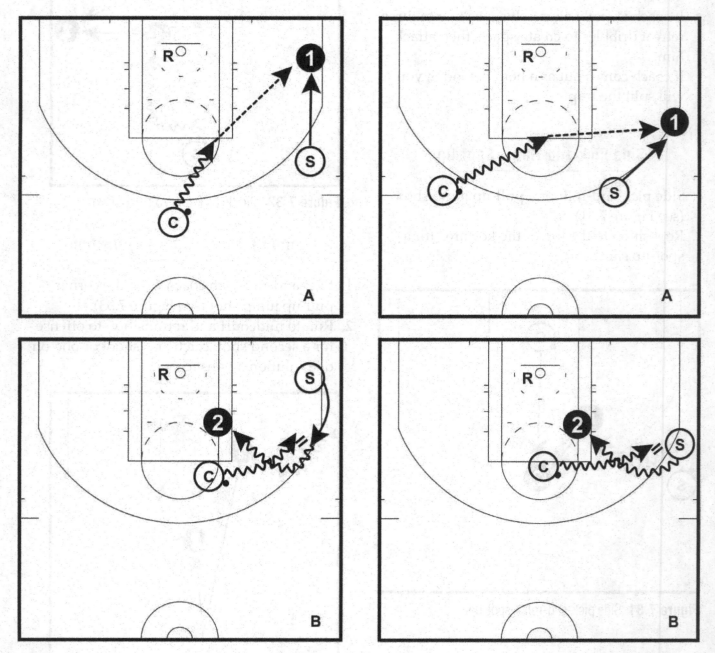

Figure 7.34 Spacing 1. One rebounder and two basketballs required.

Spacing 2

1. While coach/partner penetrates toward the middle, you move in the opposite direction, toward the elbow area to catch and shoot (see Figure 7.35).
2. Take three "slide steps" to the wing (45-degree angle) and receive a pass for a second shot.

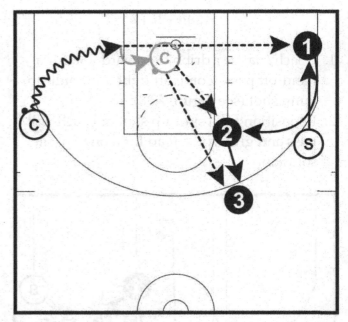

Figure 7.36 Spacing 3.

Spacing 4

1. While coach/partner penetrates toward the baseline, you move in the opposite direction, toward the top of the key area to catch and shoot (see Figure 7.37).
2. Coach will pass and give you a read for a one-on-one solution.

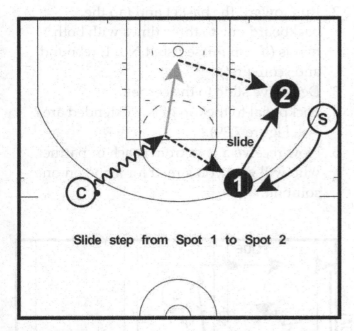

Slide step from Spot 1 to Spot 2

Figure 7.35 Spacing 2. Slide step from Spot 1 to Spot 2.

Spacing 3

1. While coach/partner penetrates toward the baseline, you drift toward the opposite corner/baseline area to catch and shoot.
2. Curl up to the elbow area for a second shot (see Figure 7.36).
3. Reposition to the top of the key area for a third shot.

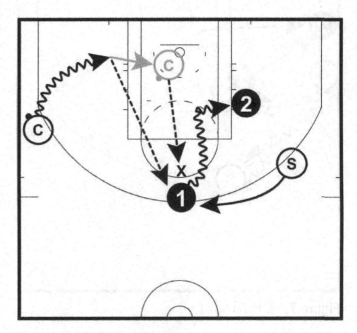

Figure 7.37 Spacing 4.

Hand Off +1

1. Coach/partner dribbles toward you for a hand-off pass. Come off tight for a pull-up jump shot (see Figure 7.38).
2. Reposition for a spot-up shot or coach will pass and give you a read for a one-on-one solution.

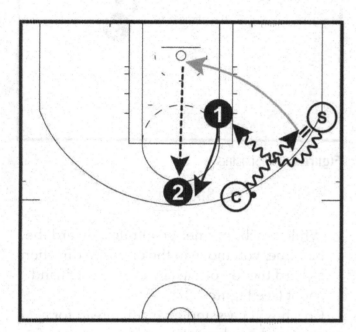

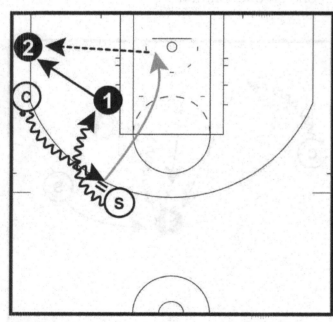

Figure 7.38 Hand off +1.

AGILITY DRILLS

These drills can be performed by perimeter and inside players.

Agility 1

1. Shot of your choice (transition, spot-up, catch and shoot, or off dribble) in top of key area.
2. Run toward the basket and tap the backboard one to three times with both hands (if you missed shot No. 1, rebound and score first).
3. Defensive slide to the corner.
4. Backpedal to the top of key extended area (see Figure 7.39).
5. Now receive a pass from coach or partner, who will give you a read for a one-on-one solution.

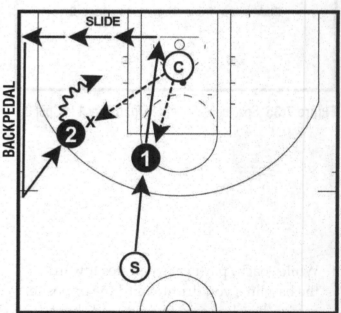

Figure 7.39 Agility 1.

Agility 2

1. Shot of your choice (transition, spot-up, catch and shoot, or off dribble) in top of key area.
2. Run toward the basket and tap the backboard one to three times with both hands (if you missed shot No. 1, rebound and score first).
3. Then defensive slide in a zigzag manner to the top of key extended area (see Figure 7.40).
4. Now receive a pass from coach or partner, who will give you a read for a one-on-one solution.

Zigzag + One-on-One

Defend on the coach or partner as he advances the ball in a zigzag manner (see Figure 7.41). When coach/partner yells "Go!" you must recover in the direction indicated (midcourt circle or either midcourt line corners) and then retransition to offense; catch the pass and go one-on-one.

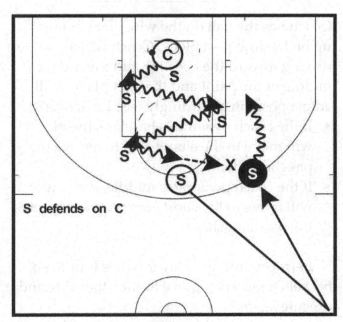

Figure 7.41 Zigzag + one-on-one.

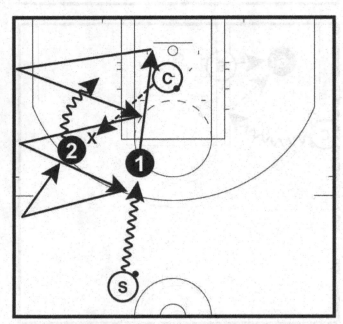

Figure 7.40 Agility 2.

INSIDE PLAYER DRILLS

Although these drills are designed for typical post players, there is no reason perimeter players cannot adapt some of the concepts and solutions to their own position drills. At the same time, post players may perform many of the previous drills.

Low-Post Spacing Drill

Coach has the ball on the wing, player posts up on the low-post block. Coach will alternate driving toward the baseline and toward the middle of the paint and the post player will adjust position accordingly (see Figure 7.42):

- If the coach penetrates baseline, the player will move to the elbow area to receive the pass and shoot.
- If the coach penetrates middle, the player will move to the short corner area to receive the pass and shoot.

Perform until the player scores four to six baskets total. Then move to the other side and execute again.

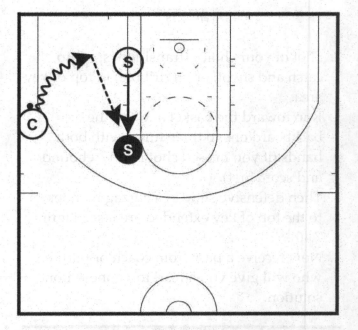

Figure 7.42 Low-post spacing drill.

Three-Shot Drill – Post

1. Reverse the ball out of the low post to the coach on the opposite wing.
2. Move to the high post area for a jump shot.
3. Then hit the low-post block, catch and shoot a turnaround jumper or perform a reverse pivot (Sikma move) and shoot.
4. Run to midcourt (alternate front run and backpedal) and retransition to offense: trailer shot, power move to the rim, or read the coach for a one-on-one solution (see Figure 7.43).

Trailer + Low-Post Move

1. Run down the middle, catch and shoot off coach/partner's pass.
2. Run toward the basket and "leg whip" as if you were cutting off your defender, then establish position on the low-post block (see Figure 7.44). Receive the pass and shoot (vary footwork and solution).

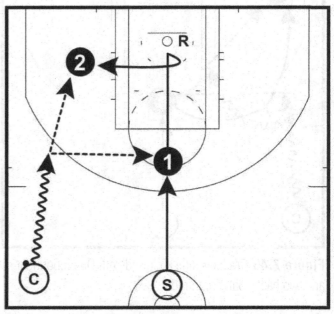

Figure 7.44 Trailer + low-post move. One rebounder and two basketballs required.

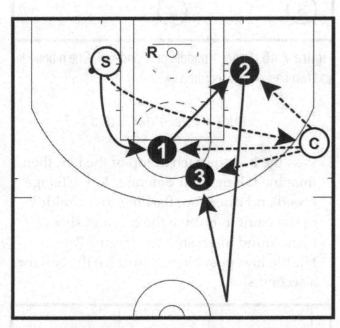

Figure 7.43 Three-shot drill – post. One rebounder and two basketballs required. Or shooter can rebound own shot and pass out to the coach.

Trailer + Side Pick-and-Roll

1. Run down the middle, catch and shoot off coach/partner's pass (see Figure 7.45).
2. Then set a ball screen for a side pick-and-roll with coach/partner; roll to the wing/baseline area for a jump shot.

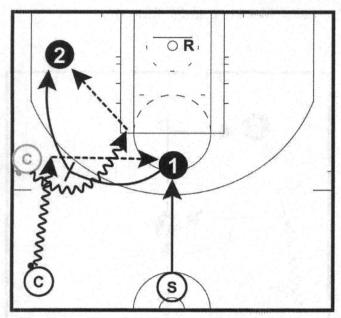

Figure 7.45 Trailer + side pick-and-roll. One rebounder and two basketballs required.

Transition + Middle Pick-and-Roll

1. Run on the wing, catch and shoot off coach/partner's pass (see Figure 7.46).
2. Then set a ball screen for a middle pick-and-roll with coach/partner; roll to the free throw line area for a jump shot.

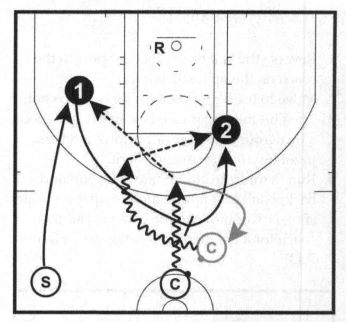

Figure 7.46 Trailer + middle pick-and-roll. One rebounder and two basketballs required.

Flash + Low-Post Move

1. Pass the ball to coach at top of the key, then imagine taking your defender low. Change speed and direction, flashing to the middle of the paint to receive the ball and shoot a turnaround jump shot (see Figure 7.47).
2. Hit the low-post block to receive the ball for a second shot.

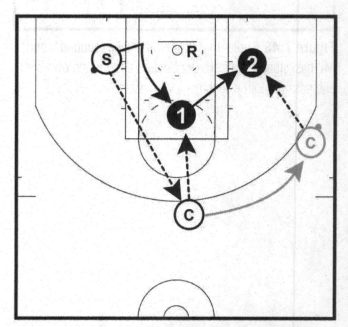

Figure 7.47 Flash + low-post move. One rebounder and two basketballs required.

High-Post + Low-Post Move

1. Catch and shoot from the high-post elbow. Vary footwork, left and right (see Figure 7.48).
2. Hit the low-post block to receive the ball with a reverse pivot and shoot (Sikma move).

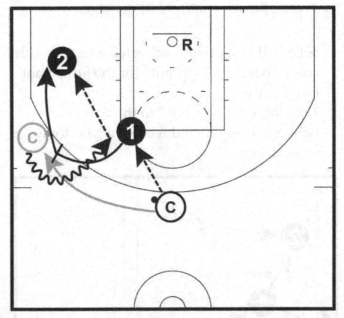

Figure 7.49 High post + pick-and-roll solution. One rebounder and two basketballs required.

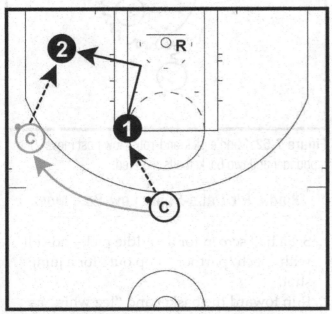

Figure 7.48 High-post + low-post move. One rebounder and two basketballs required.

Pick-and-Roll + Flash

1. Set a ball screen for a side pick-and-roll with coach/partner; roll to wing/baseline area to receive and shoot (see Figure 7.50).
2. Flash to the middle of the paint or opposite elbow for a turnaround jump shot.

High Post + Pick-and-Roll Solution

1. Catch and shoot from the high-post elbow (vary footwork, left and right).
2. Then set a ball screen for a side pick-and-roll with coach/partner: either roll to wing/baseline area to receive and shoot or "pop out" for the shot (see Figure 7.49).

Figure 7.50 Pick-and-roll + flash. One rebounder and two basketballs required.

Pick-and-Pop + Slide Step

1. Set a ball screen for a side pick-and-roll with coach/partner: "pop out" for the jump shot (see Figure 7.51).
2. Take three "slide steps" to the wing (45-degree angle) and receive a pass for a second shot.

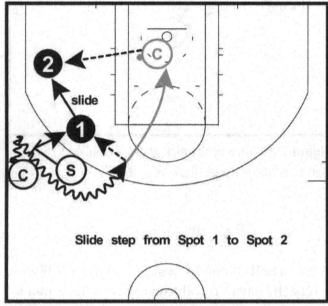

Slide step from Spot 1 to Spot 2

Figure 7.51 Pick-and-pop + slide step. One rebounder and two basketballs required.

Middle Pick-and-Roll + Low-Post Move

1. Set a ball screen for a middle pick-and-roll with coach/partner. Roll to the free throw line area for a jump shot (see Figure 7.52).
2. Hit the low-post block to receive the ball for a second shot.

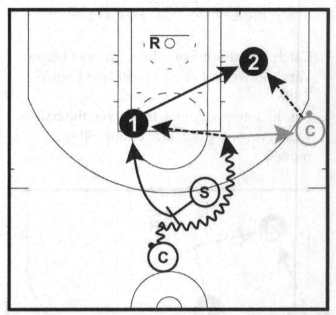

Figure 7.52 Middle pick-and-roll + low post move. One rebounder and two basketballs required.

Middle Pick-and-Pop + Low-Post Move

1. Set a ball screen for a middle pick-and-roll with coach/partner. "Pop out" for a jump shot.
2. Run toward the basket and "leg whip" as if you were cutting off your defender, then establish position on the low-post block. Receive the pass and shoot (see Figure 7.53). Vary footwork and solution.

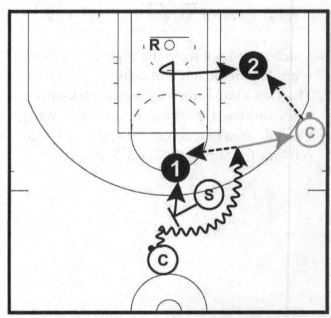

Figure 7.53 Middle pick-and-pop + low-post move. One rebounder and two basketballs required.

Wing Square Up + Flash

1. Break out to wing and receive the ball within your shooting range. Square up and shoot (see Figure 7.54).
2. Move toward the basket, then flash to the middle of the paint or opposite elbow for a turnaround jump shot.

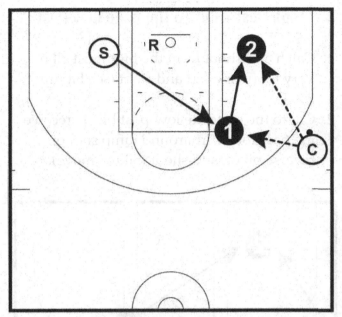

Figure 7.55 Flash to elbow + low-post move. One rebounder and two basketballs required.

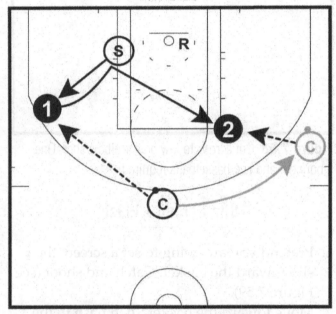

Figure 7.54 Wing square up + flash. One rebounder and two basketballs required.

Flash to Elbow + Pick-and-Roll

1. Flash from the low-post block to the opposite side elbow, receive a pass, and shoot.
2. Set a ball screen for a side pick-and-roll with coach/partner. Roll to wing/baseline area to receive and shoot (see Figure 7.56).

Flash to Elbow + Low-Post Move

1. Flash from the low-post block to the opposite side elbow, receive a pass, and shoot.
2. Hit the low-post block to receive the ball for a second shot (see Figure 7.55).

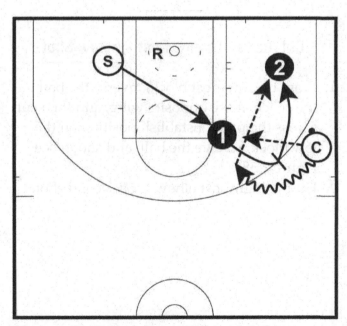

Figure 7.56 Flash to elbow + pick-and-roll. One rebounder and two basketballs required.

High Post + Cut To Opposite Low Post

1. Catch and shoot from the high-post elbow. Vary footwork, left and right (see Figure 7.57).
2. Cut to the opposite low-post block, receive the pass for a turnaround jump shot or reverse pivot, and shoot (Sikma move).

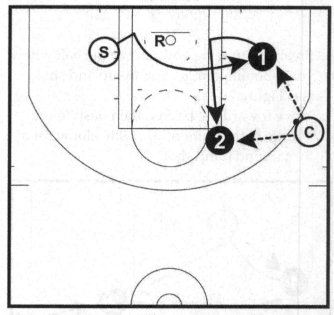

Figure 7.58 Cut across to low post + elbow shot. One rebounder and two basketballs required.

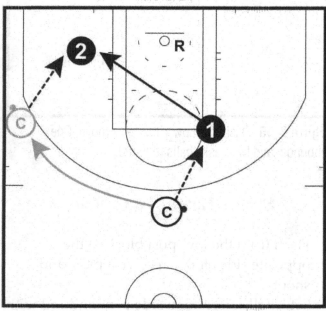

Figure 7.57 High post + cut to opposite low post. One rebounder and two basketballs required.

Slip Screen + Flash

1. Pretend you are going to set a screen, then slip toward the basket. Catch and shoot (see Figure 7.59).
2. Move toward the basket, then flash to the high post for another shot.

Cut Across To Low Post + Elbow Shot

1. From the low-post block, reverse the ball to the coach at the opposite wing, and then cut across the paint. Establish position on the low block, receive the ball, and shoot (see Figure 7.58).
2. Hit the high-post elbow for a second shot.

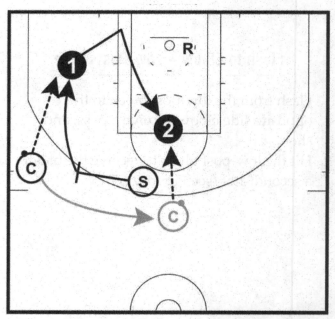

Figure 7.59 Slip screen + flash. One rebounder and two basketballs required.

About the Author

Adam Filippi is the Director of International Scouting for the World Champion Los Angeles Lakers. Before joining the Lakers in 2001, he was the youngest scout in the NBA with the New Jersey Nets in 1999. He then founded and ran Global Vision, an international scouting service that consulted with 10 NBA teams and various European clubs.

As a player development coach, Adam has worked with more than 100 NBA and overseas professional players. A Certified Personal Trainer and Performance Enhancement Specialist by the National Academy of Sports Medicine, he conducts individual training sessions, mini camps, and clinics to teach fundamental basketball skills to players of all ages and levels.